WEAPON

THE M60
MACHINE GUN

KEVIN DOCKERY

Series Editor Martin Pegler

First published in Great Britain in 2012 by Osprey Publishing,
Midland House, West Way, Botley, Oxford, OX2 0PH, UK
44-02 23rd Street, Suite 219, Long Island City, NY 11101, USA

E-mail: info@ospreypublishing.com

Osprey Publishing is part of the Osprey Group

A CIP catalog record for this book is available from the
British Library

Print ISBN: 978 1 84908 844 2

PDF ebook ISBN: 978 1 84908 845 9

ePub ebook ISBN: 978 1 78200 326 7

Page layout by Mark Holt

Index by Rob Munro

Battlescene artwork by Mark Stacey

Cutaway by Alan Gilliland

Typeset in Sabon and Univers

Originated by PDQ Media, Bungay, UK

Printed in China through Worldprint Ltd.

12 13 14 15 16   10 9 8 7 6 5 4 3 2 1

Osprey Publishing is supporting the Woodland Trust, the UK's
leading woodland conservation charity, by funding the dedication
of trees.

Artist's acknowledgment

Mark Stacey would like to thank Captain Peter Laidler of the
Small Arms School Corps, Warminster, UK, for generously
allowing him to photograph M60s in their collection.

Cover images courtesy US Department of Defense and US Navy.

CONTENTS

INTRODUCTION

There are few military small arms that elicit the range of feelings and opinions evoked by the M60 light machine gun (LMG). It has been loved by some of the men who have carried it, and just as strongly despised by others. Each side of the argument will have facts to back up their opinions, sometimes tempered with personal experience.

An entire generation of American soldiers knew of only one man-portable machine gun in the arms room. That weapon was the M60 – also called, affectionately or heatedly, "the Pig." For the US forces that fought in Southeast Asia, "humping the Pig" meant carrying the M60 machine gun through Vietnam's jungles, rice paddies, and waterways, and up its hills. Somehow, when you carried that substantial chunk of metal and rubber in your arms or across your shoulders, the terrain always seemed to be uphill, or always troubled by mud and water. Yet the M60 could also make you feel like Mars, the God of War himself, when you used it.

A good man with an M60 was worth his weight in gold in a combat situation. He could be the most popular man in a firefight, swinging that big weapon into play and cutting apart the landscape to get at the enemy. And the M60 gunner could also be the most unpopular individual, the person you least wanted to be anywhere near in that same firefight. For the power of the M60 was well known on both sides of the battlefield. When the thunder of that big weapon opened up, it was instantly recognizable. The M60 was the gun the enemy wanted to silence first, so the weapon drew fire as well as put it out.

In combat, where the M16 and the AK-47 were the most common weapons in the fight, the power of the M60's big 7.62mm NATO (North Atlantic Treaty Organization) round would put the others to shame when it came to penetration of cover and elimination of a target. Yet that same ammunition was heavy, and without it, the M60 was nothing more than a large, very clumsy club. Everyone in the squad would carry a supply of ammunition for the M60 when they were asked, or told, by the sergeant. Getting rid of that ammunition by handing it over to the gunner or the assistant gunner as soon as possible was also a very popular activity. But the Pig commanded respect, and it had to be fed.

In the defense, the M60 could be put into position quickly to command a very large field of fire. Using the tripod made it a particularly effective weapon at night, with pre-planned fields of fire "dialed in" by the gunner. A good M60 crew, comprised of a gunner and assistant gunner, could keep an M60 operating for an extended length of time as long as they had a sufficient supply of ammunition and made effective barrel changes. Locked into position, the M60 could cover a specific avenue of approach and made the frontline immediately lethal to anyone who tried to cross it.

During Operation *Mokuleia* in South Vietnam in 1966, a soldier of the 27th Infantry Regiment moves as part of a patrol walking along a rice paddy dike. With belts of ammunition festooned across both his shoulders, and belt bandoleers of more ammunition hanging at his waist, he is heavily burdened. If he has to fire the M60 cradled in his arms, the weight of the ammunition will seem like nothing. He is well prepared to put out heavy fire from his machine gun to support his brother soldiers in the patrol. (NARA)

Supporting an attack, the M60 was equally commanding. Set up on a tripod, or even on its integral bipod, a properly placed M60 could lay down a heavy covering fire, allowing troops to move forward while the enemy kept their heads down. And the M60 could be snatched up and moved forward, the gun keeping up with the troops as necessary. It was not hard to pick up the M60 and shoulder it like a rifle when necessary. It therefore could be fired from the shoulder, or more easily from the hip, as the gunner moved forward during the assault.

The author first experienced the M60 machine gun during basic training, along with many other volunteers and draftees in the US Army, in the final years of the Vietnam conflict. During basic training, instruction on the M60 was limited, but I remember being more than impressed. Later training, as an armorer and in the infantry, resulted in much greater exposure to the weapon. My job was to keep the M60s assigned to my company operating, which meant performing maintenance and sourcing spare parts.

Much of the hatred some soldiers had towards the M60 was a result of worn weapons or, in some cases, a lack of maintenance and training. Kept clean and in good repair, the gun worked, and it worked well.

During a field exercise in 1972, this member of the 101st Airborne Division holds his M60 machine gun in the ready position. The weapon had been the mainstay light machine gun used by all US forces during the Vietnam War and it was still going to serve in frontline duty for several decades after this picture was taken. (US Department of Defense)

It was accurate and powerful, a fine combination of traits for an infantry weapon. Admittedly it was temperamental, and there were definite flaws in its design, but it was the weapon issued, and it was paid dividends to learn how to use it properly.

As the primary 7.62mm machine gun in US service, the M60 was modified and changed to fit certain applications. It became the primary automatic weapon on a huge number of helicopter gunships. It was, and still is, a common sight on US Navy small craft. The M60 was modified to be remotely fired and mounted on vehicles. Improved and developed, the newest version of the M60 machine gun, the M60E4, has been used by some of the US military's most elite forces.

The legendary Browning .30-cal machine guns endured in US service for 40 years. They were heavy and clumsy to use in some situations, but were well thought of by the men who pulled the triggers. The M60 family of weapons lasted nearly as long – 38 years in frontline US service. Some special operations forces (SOF) used modernized M60s well into the "War on Terror" (2001 onward). Production of new weapons continues. A number of foreign governments are still purchasing US-made M60 machine guns in the newest configurations, and even some US forces have recently bought M60s for applications where it is just considered better than the present-issue weapons.

Loved and hated, the M60 has been serving for over half a century, and it isn't done firing yet.

A very heavily armed trooper maintains watch in 2004 while guarding a convoy through a mountain pass in Afghanistan. In front of him is a mounted M60 machine gun. To his right is a strapped-down M134 AT4 antitank weapon, and behind him can be seen part of the receiver of a Mark 19 Mod 3 40mm grenade launcher. (US Department of Defense)

DEVELOPMENT
The long road to the M60

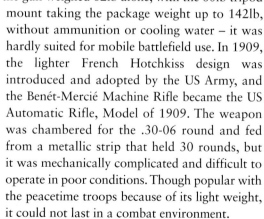

With Lt Kirkland at the controls of the Type B Wright pusher plane, Capt Charles DeForest Chandler cradles a Model 1911 Lewis gun in his lap. On June 7, 1912, Capt Chandler became the first person to fire a machine gun from an aircraft in flight. (US Navy)

THE AMERICAN MACHINE-GUN EXPERIENCE

At the beginning of the 20th century, the conceptual use of the machine gun still hadn't been thought through by the US military. The Gatling gun had been used as a portable piece of artillery, not as a tactical machine gun, and the later self-loading options had their fair share of problems. The .30-03 Model 1904 Maxim gun, an early US adoption of the Maxim, worked dependably, but the gun weighed 62lb alone, with the 80lb tripod mount taking the package weight up to 142lb, without ammunition or cooling water – it was hardly suited for mobile battlefield use. In 1909, the lighter French Hotchkiss design was introduced and adopted by the US Army, and the Benét-Mercié Machine Rifle became the US Automatic Rifle, Model of 1909. The weapon was chambered for the .30-06 round and fed from a metallic strip that held 30 rounds, but it was mechanically complicated and difficult to operate in poor conditions. Though popular with the peacetime troops because of its light weight, it could not last in a combat environment.

The gas-operated Lewis gun, however, offered a far more satisfying proposition, with a top-mounted pan magazine and thick air-cooled barrel. Designed by an Army officer, Major Isaac Newton Lewis, the Lewis gun made its first firing appearance in 1911. The weapon was relatively light, handy, and could fire the .30-06 cartridge

accurately at a cyclic rate of 750 rounds per minute (rpm). Yet for a number of political and financial reasons, the Lewis gun was not commercially successful with the US forces. Taking his weapon with him, therefore, Lewis went to England and Europe where the gun was more enthusiastically received. The upshot was that instead of having Lewis guns, the US Marines entered combat in 1917 with the French Model 1915 Chauchat LMG, considered by just about everyone to be one of the worst machine-gun designs ever produced. The Marines wouldn't get their Lewis guns back until after World War I, but by that time another weapons designer had established his guns as among the best of their kind in the world.

For close to half a century, beginning in World War I, the US military depended on one kind of machine gun, designed by the great John Moses Browning. The basic M1917 (water-cooled) and M1919 (air-cooled) machine guns were considered utterly dependable and capable of amazing acts of endurance. On February 27, 1917, John Browning took his new Browning Automatic Rifle (BAR) and the water-cooled machine gun to Congress Heights in Washington, DC. There, he demonstrated the weapons to the military, members of Congress, foreign representatives,

The French M1915 Chauchat machine gun. The specimen here is missing the bipod legs, normally held by the small bracket at the front of the receiver. The sharply curved magazine was necessary due to the French 8mm Lebel cartridge fired by the Chauchat having a steep taper to the cartridge case. To see how many rounds remained in the weapon, the side of the magazine is cut away. This exposed the rounds to the dirt and mud of the trenches, adding to the jamming problem that contributed to the Chauchat's terrible reputation for dependable operation. (Smithsonian Institution)

The Model 1917 Browning water-cooled .30-cal machine gun on its heavy, fully adjustable tripod. (Smithsonian Institution)

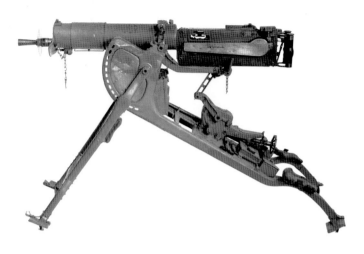

and the press. The weapons were impressive, but initially there was only a limited amount of funds allocated to the adoption of new machine guns.

The demand for a new machine gun for the US Army increased dramatically when the United States declared war on Germany on April 6, 1917. The military took a fresh look at the Browning water-cooled gun, and adopted it officially. Nearly 43,000 M1917 guns were produced by the end of World War I, by three manufacturers. The weapons arrived too late to have much effect on the war effort, but they established a place for themselves as the premier .30-cal heavy machine guns (HMGs) in US hands. Another very popular Browning design also made its first appearance during World War I – the M1918 BAR. The later M1918A2 BAR became the mainstay US squad automatic rifle of World War II and the Korean War. The 20lb weapon fed from a 20-round magazine, and saw action in every theater of war involving US forces well into the 1950s. It also ably demonstrated the tactical value of a dependable automatic weapon that could be carried and operated by one man.

The basic design of the Browning M1917 was quickly modified from the water-cooled system to an air-cooled one for possible use in aircraft during World War I. Another application for an air-cooled Browning was as a tank-mounted machine gun. The M1919 design was ready for issue just one week too late to see action during World War I, but the design was developed further over the coming decades. Finally, modified with a 24in long barrel, perforated air-cooling jacket, and reinforced receiver points, the M1919A4 LMG was officially adopted by the US Army in 1935. Yet it was not a true LMG – the M1919A4 was recognized as being too large and heavy to be employed properly by one man, one of the key LMG criteria. In 1939, therefore, the US Army Ordnance Department recommended that a new LMG be developed and adopted. The specifications put forth for the new weapon were that it be air-cooled, capable of semi- and full-automatic fire, weigh not more than 22lb, and be no longer than 36in. The weapon was also to be capable of firing five 100-round bursts in five minutes.

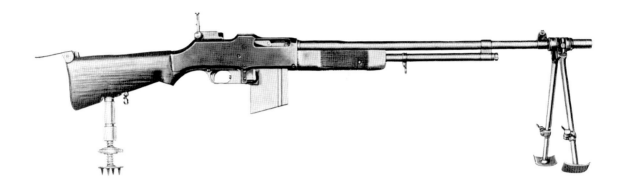

More than a half-dozen weapons were developed for the LMG program, slowed by the entry of the United States into World War II at the end of 1941. There was even a belt-fed conversion of the BAR produced for the program. The only problem was that none of the weapons could fulfill all of the requirements for a satisfactory, rugged, and dependable weapon. Some months before the competition of the LMG program commenced, another weapon began development – a "lightened" M1919A4 Browning intended to be usable by one man. To make the new Browning modification, a shoulder stock and bipod were added to the basic weapon. Some parts of the basic design were lightened, particularly the barrel, and a carrying handle added. In February 1943, the new Browning M1919A6 LMG was recommended for adoption to meet the needs of the frontline US infantryman.

The M1918A2 Browning Automatic Rifle, complete with the rarely seen rear monopod. This variation of the BAR was the most prevalent model used by all US forces during World War II and the Korean War. The weapon was heavy but extremely strong, being made almost entirely of machined steel components. The bipod at the front of the weapon could be, and often was, easily removed by the user. (US Army)

THE GERMAN DESIGNS

In Europe, a very different evolution was taking place in terms of machine-gun design. What the post-World War I German military wanted was a "universal machine gun," one that could be carried and employed by one soldier on the assault, usable as a medium machine gun (MMG) from a mount or bipod, capable of sustained firing as an HMG when necessary, and applicable as an antiaircraft gun. It took the German ordnance designers nearly 15 years to come up with the groundbreaking design that fulfilled these criteria.

The *Maschinengewehr 34* or MG 34 introduced a whole new concept in machine guns. The long, cylindrical weapon had a removable bipod and was used easily by one man. A small magazine made to hold a single 50-round length of ammunition belt could be attached to the side of the receiver so the weapon could be carried and employed almost as an automatic rifle. A complex tripod enabled the gun to be employed for long-range sustained fire, also facilitated by a quick-change barrel – after about 250 rounds had been fired, the hot barrel could be changed for a cool one and fire continued. A tall antiaircraft tripod allowed the MG 34 to engage low-flying aircraft. The military intent was that every infantry squad – consisting of a squad leader and nine men – be equipped with an MG 34.

The MG 34 light machine gun. A carefully crafted weapon, the MG 34 is primarily made of finely machined parts. The spare barrel is shown underneath the weapon. (US Army)

The MG 34 on the complex Lafette 34 tripod. The tripod is fitted with an optical periscope sight, visible to the left of the gun just in front of the rear of the butt stock. The barrel carrier shown underneath the tripod holds two barrels. (US Army)

A standard machine gun of the German military throughout World War II, the MG 34 demonstrated the success of the universal-machine-gun concept. The general-purpose MG 34 did have several weaknesses in its design, though. It was constructed primarily of carefully machined parts, fitted together by skilled labor. The complex trigger mechanism allowed semi-automatic fire when the top of the trigger was pulled, and full-automatic fire when the bottom of the trigger was pulled. Such complexity and fine machining was not helpful for a weapon that had to be made in the many thousands under wartime conditions. Hence by 1942, the German war machine had brought a new machine gun onto the battlefield – the MG 42.

The MG 42 was rugged, relatively light, and very fast to manufacture. Gone were the carefully machined surfaces of the MG 34 – in their place came stamped metal. The long barrel could still be changed quickly and efficiently when it became hot, and the barrel of the MG 42 could heat up

fast – with some ammunition, the cyclic rate could reach 1,350rpm and more. This made the MG 42 wasteful of ammunition unless handled by a disciplined and experienced gunner. On the other hand, the rate of fire from "Hitler's Buzzsaw" proved terrifying to the Allied troops who had to face it for the first time. It was considered one of the finest machine guns to come out of World War II.

By February 1943, US ordnance authorities released their first report on the MG 42, following testing of a captured example. The barrel-change system and the belt-feed mechanism were considered some of the best features of the design, and a decision was made to convert several MG 42s to fire American .30-cal M2 ammunition. The Saginaw Steering Gear Division of General Motors received the contract to convert two MG 42s, which were ready to be test-fired by October 1943. The converted weapons, called the T24, proved a major disappointment. At Aberdeen Proving Ground, Maryland, the T24 could not be made to function properly. Gunners eventually managed to fire a complete 100-round belt, but only by firing in two- and three-shot bursts. The tests were suspended after just 1,583 rounds were fired; 51 malfunctions occurred during the test. It was later found that there had been a conversion error in changing the guns over from the German 7.92×57mm round to the American .30-cal M2 (7.62×63mm round). The nearly quarter of an inch difference in lengths between the two rounds of ammunition had not been accounted for in some parts of the conversion. The American ammunition was just too long to properly eject and clear the receiver. The T24 project was abandoned and the weapons shelved.

The MG 34 and MG 42 were not the only influential German machine guns of World War II. Another LMG demonstrated a very advanced

The MG 42 machine gun. The receiver is made up of sheet metal stampings welded together. Relatively light and easy to handle, the weapon was known for its very high rate of fire, described as the sound of "ripping canvas" by soldiers who faced it. The large rectangular handle sticking out from the right side of the receiver is the cocking handle for the bolt. (Smithsonian Institution)

The T24 machine gun mounted on an M2 tripod. The pintle mount at the front of the weapon was specially made for this adaptation while the rear T&E gear is simply modified from the standard mount used with the M1919A4 machine gun. The leaf of the rear sight has been raised for more accurate aiming. (US Government)

A left-side view of the FG 42 Ausf. G light machine gun/rifle. The 20-round magazine for the weapon is lying in the center foreground. The magazine well is visible on the receiver above the pistol grip. The bolt is in the forward position and the cam slot to rotate the bolt can be seen. The long, thin rod underneath the barrel is the cruciform bayonet stowed in the carrying position. The tip of the bayonet is centered on the front of the gas system plug. For use, the bayonet would be reversed and the cylindrical end section, underneath the muzzle in this picture, would be locked into the joint between the top of the unfolded bipod legs. (US Army)

concept, in spite of using aspects of earlier guns. Following the harrowing experience of combat during the invasion of Crete in 1941, the German *Fallschirmjäger* (paratroops) requested a weapon that would be lightweight, capable of full- and semi-automatic fire, have limited capability as an LMG and be applicable to sniper roles. In about 18 months, Rheinmetall and Kreighoff both had prototypes available. The design accepted by the German Air Force was the Rheinmetall submission by gunmaker Louis Stang. As a political action Hermann Göring, the head of the *Luftwaffe*, personally showed the weapon to Hitler, who was so impressed that the first 17 FG 42s produced were issued to Hitler's personal bodyguard. The weapon was never manufactured in very large numbers, however, but the unique aspects of the FG 42 caused the weapon to leave a great impression on a number of ordnance personnel, including those in the United States.

The basic design of the FG 42 has the weapon feeding from a side-mounted (left side) magazine, an arrangement that lets the gunner maintain a very low profile when shooting from the prone position. Another of the special features of the FG 42 is that the operating rod, bolt, and trigger system fires the gun from closed bolt for accurate semi-automatic fire, but from the open-bolt position when it is set on full-automatic. The closed bolt means that the bolt is fully forward and locked to the breech when the gun is ready to fire – only the firing pin moves when the trigger is pulled, meaning that there is no shift in bolt mass to affect aim. Open-bolt firing means that the entire bolt is held to the rear by the sear mechanism and released by the trigger. The bolt goes forward and feeds the round into the chamber when the trigger is pulled, firing the chambered round when it is fully seated. The open-bolt feature helps air cool the weapon more efficiently during full-automatic fire, but the shift in bolt mass makes the firing less accurate.

The adoption of basic design characteristics from other weapons, such as the American Johnson M1941 and Lewis gun, enabled the FG 42 to be developed in a relatively short time. That short development period, combined with the fact that Germany was fully at war, caused the FG 42 to see combat before it was fully "debugged." Primarily made by Krieghoff Waffenfabrik of Suhl, the FG 42 Ausf. G was the last and most improved of its type. One of the improvements to the weapon was the addition of a gas regulator to the system, which allowed the gas system to be adjusted to operate most effectively using different types (and quality) of ammunition. It also allowed the operator to increase the amount of gas entering the system when using the gun in difficult environments, such as extreme cold or mud. The strange-looking but efficient muzzle brake (copied in part from the MG 42) and buffered butt stock made the FG 42 Ausf. G relatively comfortable to shoot, and accurate even when firing bursts on full-automatic. Fewer than 7,000 of all types of the FG 42 design were made during the war, but they had a lasting effect on the firearms world well out of proportion to their numbers. The weapon was one of the first assault rifles chambered for a "full-size" rifle cartridge.

Precursors to the M60

Name	Caliber	Overall length	Barrel length	Empty weight	Feed device (weight)	Cyclic rate of fire	Mount (weight)
M1917 Lewis	.30.06-cal M2 (7.62×63mm)	51in (129.5cm)	26.63in (67.6cm)	26.5lb (12.02kg)	47-rd removable pan magazine (4.16lb/1.89kg)	550rpm	Shoulder or bipod fired; removable bipod (1.75lb/0.79kg)
M1918A2 BAR	.30.06-cal M2 (7.62×63mm)	47.18in (119.8cm)	24in (61cm)	16.31lb (7.4kg)	20-rd removable box magazine (1.44lb/0.65kg)	500–650rpm fast; 300–450rpm slow	Shoulder or bipod fired; removable bipod (2.44lb/1.11kg)
Browning M1917A1	.30.06-cal M2 (7.62×63mm)	38.5in (97.8cm)	24in (61cm)	32.63lb (14.8kg)*	250-rd M1917 fabric belt (14.54lb/6.60kg)	450–600rpm	Tripod fired; M1917 tripod with cradle (52.3lb/24.13kg)
Browning M1919A4	.30.06-cal M2 (7.62×63mm)	48in (121.9cm)	24in (61cm)	31lb (14.06kg)	250-rd M1 link belt (16.61lb/7.53kg)	550–650rpm	Tripod fired; M2 tripod with T&E mechanism and pintle (16.5lb/7.48kg)
Browning M1919A6	.30.06-cal M2 (7.62×63mm)	53in (134.6cm)**	24in (61cm)	33.5lb (15.2kg)	250-rd M1 link belt (16.61lb/7.53kg)	600–675rpm	Shoulder or bipod fired; removable M1919A6 bipod (3.32lb/1.51kg)
MG 34	8mm Mauser (7.92×57mm)	48.25in (122.6cm)	24.5in (62.2cm)	26.75lb (12.13kg)	50-rd section of Gurt 34 link belt (1.72lb/0.78kg)	800–900rpm	Shoulder, bipod, or tripod fired; removable bipod (2.5lb/1.13kg), or Lafette 34 tripod (52.03lb/23.6kg)
MG 42	8mm Mauser (7.92×57mm)	48.13in (122.3cm)	20.81in (52.9cm)	25.71lb (11.66kg)	50-rd section of Gurt 34 link belt (1.72lb/0.78kg)	1,200–1,350rpm	Shoulder, bipod, or tripod fired; removable bipod (2.46lb/1.12kg), or Lafette 42 tripod (45.2lb/20.5kg)
FG 42 Ausf. G	8mm Mauser (7.92×57mm)	38.4in (97.5cm)	19.7in (50cm)	10.9lb (4.95kg)†	20-rd box magazine (2lb/0.91kg)	750rpm	Shoulder or bipod fired; integral bipod

* without water; 39.93lb (18.11kg) with 7 pints (3.31l) water   ** including M7 flash hider and shoulder stock   † including integral bipod

THE POSTWAR YEARS

Soon after the war had ended, both in the Pacific as well as Europe, the Chief of US Army Ordnance research and development, Col René R. Studler, wanted a comprehensive examination of the revolutionary German FG 42. To conduct the study, Studler had three of the best examples of the FG 42 Ausf. G made available to Aberdeen Proving Grounds. In 1946, three weapons were delivered to the Proving Grounds and put through the official Standard Automatic Rifle Test.

The FG 42 was a hybrid, a rifle-sized weapon capable of acting as an LMG. The tests showed that the design came very close to meeting this description. Most astonishing was how controllable the weapon was on full-auto fire. At 50yd, firing in five- to ten-round bursts with iron sights from the prone position, the FG 42 kept its rounds in a circle slightly less than 10in across. Accuracy was expected to be even better when the guns were tested with their telescopic sights, but the captured sights were damaged and the tests with them were inconclusive.

The basic result of the examination was to recommend that several versions of the FG 42 be built to chamber the .30-cal M2 round, and further testing continued. This conversion was not done, even though some aspects of the FG 42 were superior to the American weapons being developed – that series resulting in the M14 rifle. But the capabilities of the FG 42 were not lost on Col Studler.

The T44 light machine gun, a combination of the FG 42 and the belt feed of an MG 42. The weapon has been heavily modified to allow the belt feed to be incorporated into the system. The feed cover is open and a loaded belt in the feed tray. The empty portion of the non-disintegrating belt comes out of the top of the weapon and is hanging down the right side in this picture. The rear sight of the FG 42 was removed for this conversion. (Springfield Armory National Historical Site)

The T44

The FG 42 could act as a machine gun, but only as long as its 20-round magazine held ammunition. A belt-feed system was preferred by the US military for an LMG, and the Germans had developed an excellent one for the MG 42, plus the stamped sheet-metal design of both the FG 42 and the MG 42 allowed the weapons to be mass produced easily, particularly in the United States where formed sheet-metal production had been raised to a high art by the automotive industry. The Ordnance Corps R&D section, under the direction of Col Studler, directed that the FG 42 be mated with the belt-feed mechanism of the MG 42.

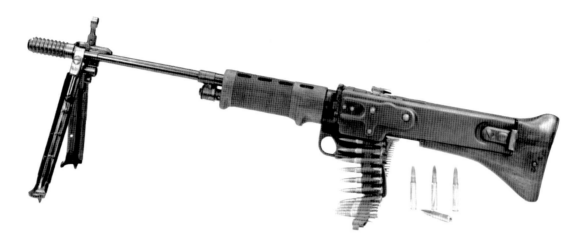

In June 1946, the work for the conversion was contracted to the Engineering Division of the Bridge Tool & Die Works, Philadelphia, Pennsylvania. The mechanical conversion of the base weapon was completed in December 1946, and the resulting design was referred to as the T44 LMG. The weapon had a very unusual appearance; it was only intended to prove the idea of a very lightweight belt-fed machine gun. The T44 couldn't be aimed properly, the rear sight of the FG 42 having been removed for the conversion and the left side of the receiver cut away and modified. A bearing stud had been added to the rear of the bolt to operate the belt-feed mechanism. The complete feed cover of an MG 42 was attached to the left side of the weapon, the feeding arrangement for the belt having the belt come up from the bottom of the weapon and the empty section of the non-disintegrating link belt extend out the top of the gun and down the right side. Ejection of the empty casings was out the right side of the weapon through the existing ejection port.

To prevent a repeat of the disastrous showing of the T24 weapon, and to simplify the conversion, the T44 remained chambered for the original FG 42 cartridge, the 7.92×57mm round. American ammunition of known quality and characteristics was used for the firing tests. Shoulder-firing the T44 was possible, and the weapon remained controllable. The in-line design of the FG 42 lined the barrel up with the shoulder stock, and therefore recoil went straight back into the shooter's shoulder. That configuration helped keep the weapon in line with the target, even when firing on full automatic.

The T44 provided a very successful demonstration of the idea of a belt-fed FG 42, despite a few problems. One problem was that the light barrel of the base weapon overheated quickly from extended firing. Another was that the light weapon recoiled and shook badly on full-auto when it was fired without the muzzle brake installed. With the muzzle brake, the T44 was easily controllable and very quick to handle.

The T52 series

The T44 project came about in part because of recommendations the Army Ground Forces Equipment Board made in 1945, when it was apparent that the war would soon be over. The board made a study of what would be needed by the postwar military in the way of development programs. Their recommendation for a machine gun to replace existing .30-cal models stated that the new weapon should weigh about 20lb, have a maximum effective range of 1,000yd, and have selective rates of fire of 600 and 1,200rpm. In 1946 the War Department Equipment Board reported on their deeper examination of the question of future weapons development. Recommendations from the board took into account the deficiencies with existing American weapons. The main question to be answered: what would it take to ensure that American weapons and armor were significantly superior to those of any potential future enemy?

The results of the new board were ready in May 1946. One set of their findings took the requirements of the earlier board for a new machine gun and changed the maximum effective range to 1,800yd, added the specifications of a quick-change barrel, disintegrating-belt feed, flash hider, and a bipod and tripod that were as light as practicable. To meet these requirements meant a change to the design of the T44. That new weapon was the T52. The Bridge Tool & Die Works were contracted to continue their development of the combined FG 42/MG 42 in the T52 series. Initial testing of the new weapon was completed and the report published in October 1948.

The T52 was a more extensive modification of an existing FG 42. The MG 42 feed cover was added to the top of the T52 in a more conventional configuration. To operate the feed system, an extending lug was attached to the rear of the operating rod rather than the bolt. A quick-change barrel with a flash hider was added to the system – now a hot barrel could be removed and another installed in its place. The locking lugs for the bolt were moved from the receiver to the barrel, giving the barrel a fixed headspace with the bolt. The weapon was chambered for the T65E1 cartridge, a 7.62mm round with a 1.95in-long case. Ammunition was fed into the gun carried by a disintegrating-link belt made from push-through T55 links.

The T55 belt link assembled into a belt section. The rounds being inserted show how the ammunition holds the belt together. The open bottom of the link, seen in the end view of a link to the left of the belt, allows the ammunition to be stripped from the front of the link – pushed out of the belt as the bolt moves forward. (US Government)

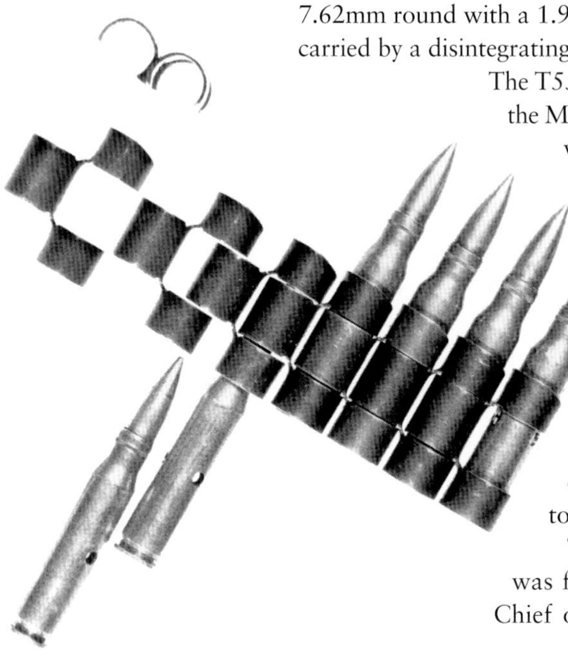

The T55 link was based in part on the German belts for the MG 34 and MG 42. To feed the round, the cartridge was pushed forward by the bolt, stripping it out of the link. Once the ammunition was out of the link, the link disconnected from the rest of the belt and was ejected out of the gun. Prior to the new link design, all other belt-fed US .30-cal machine guns were loaded with links that had to have the round pulled out from the back to feed into the weapon. Many of the belts used during World War II were still non-disintegrating cloth belts, a design that dated back to before World War I.

The new T52 showed further promise, but it was far from a finalized weapon. The Office of the Chief of Ordnance requested various modifications.

Experimental variants

Name	Caliber	Overall length	Barrel length	Empty weight	Feed device (weight)	Cyclic rate of fire	Mount (weight)
T24	.30.06-cal M2 (7.62×63mm)	46.88in (119.1cm)	20.81in (52.9cm)	24.38lb (11.06kg)	50-rd section of Gurt 34 link belt (3.15lb/1.43kg)	614rpm	Shoulder, bipod, or tripod fired; removable bipod (2.67lb/1.21kg), or M2 tripod with T&E mechanism and pintle (15.3lb/6.94kg)
T44	8mm Mauser (7.92×57mm)	39in (99cm)	19.5in (49.5cm)	14lb (6.35kg)	50-rd section of Gurt 34 link belt (3.15lb/1.43kg)	500rpm	Shoulder or bipod fired; integral bipod
T52	7.62mm T65E3	39.13in (99.1cm)	20in (50.8cm)	16.25lb (7.37kg)	T55 link	575rpm	Shoulder, bipod, or tripod fired; integral bipod, or T113 tripod
T52E1	7.62mm T65E1	41.75in (106cm)	22in (55.9cm)	17.75lb (8.05kg)	T55 link	650rpm	Shoulder, bipod, or tripod fired; removable bipod, or T113E1 tripod
T52E2	7.62mm T65E3	39.25in (99.7cm)	22in (55.9cm)	17.75lb (8.05kg)	T55 link	700rpm	Shoulder, bipod, or tripod fired; removable bipod, or T113E1 tripod
T52E3	7.62mm T65E3	43.5in (110.5cm)	22in (55.9cm)	18.5lb (8.39kg)	T55 link	700rpm	Shoulder, bipod, or tripod fired; integral bipod, or M74 tripod with adaptor
T52E4	7.62mm NATO (7.62×51mm)	44.5in (113cm)	22in (55.9cm)	20lb (9.07kg)	T89 link	625rpm	Shoulder, bipod, or tripod fired; integral bipod,or T178 tripod (25lb/11.34kg)
T52E5	7.62mm NATO (7.62×51mm)	45.25in (114.9cm)	22in (55.9cm)	23.5lb (10.66kg)	T89 link	550rpm	Shoulder, bipod, or tripod fired; integral bipod, or T178 tripod (25lb/11.34kg)
T161	.30.06-cal M2 (7.62×63mm)	Weapon never completed in this caliber					
T161E1	7.62mm T65E3	43.5in (110.5cm)	22in (55.9cm)	23.93lb (10.85kg)	T55 link	500rpm	Shoulder, bipod, or tripod fired; integral bipod, or T178 tripod (25lb/11.34kg), or T182 tripod
T161E2	7.62mm T65E3	43in (109.2cm)	22in (55.9cm)	23lb (10.43kg)	T89 link	550rpm	Shoulder, bipod, or tripod fired; integral bipod, or T178 tripod (25lb/11.34kg), or T182 tripod
T161E3	7.62mm NATO (7.62×51mm)	43.5in (110.5cm)	22in (55.9cm)	24.5lb (11.11kg)	M13 link	500–650rpm	Shoulder, bipod, or tripod fired; integral bipod; M91 tripod (24.6lb/11.11kg), or M122 tripod with pintle and T&E gear (19.5lb/8.85kg)

In December 1949, the report on the development of the T52E1 was released. One of the major changes in the E1 weapon was the further evolution of the new style of gas system. The original T44 used the gas-impingement system, in which propellant gas is tapped from the barrel through a small hole, where it can act on a piston connected to the operating rod. This system is commonly used in a large number of gas-operated weapons.

The T52 series used the gas-expansion system of operating. In this system, the propellant gas is tapped from the barrel in the usual manner. But instead of just acting on the face of the piston, the gas expands into a hollow piston with an open front and through it into the gas cylinder. The rear of the gas piston has a series of holes around it that line up with the gas port to allow the gas to enter the system. When the gas pressure has reached a point that it can overcome the resistance of the operating system, the piston moves to the rear; the holes move out of line with the gas port, cutting off the flow of any further propellant gas from entering. The hot gases expand, continuing to do work on the piston, forcing it back to work the action. Excess pressure is bled off through a vent.

The gas-expansion system makes for a very smooth, consistent operating force. It is also very hard to adjust the system to operate with more propellant gas if the weapon is dirty or operating in a harsh climate. In the new design the gas system attached to the barrel assembly and was changed with the barrel; changing the barrel to a fresh one gave the

US designations

Pieces of military equipment undergo a number of designator changes as they are developed. Experimental materials are designated by T-numbers, with a capital "T" in front of Arabic numerals to indicate the specific design being produced. For the developmental series that led to the M60, the first weapon was designated the "Gun, Machine, T52." As development continues, modifications in the design add an "E" suffix to the designation, followed by an Arabic numeral to indicate the sequence of the accumulative changes. The adoption of modifications to the design resulted in the new designator "Gun, Machine T52E1." The final number increases with the continuing adoption of modifications to the original design.

Once an experimental or developmental device has passed testing and is considered for official standardization for military issue, it receives a new designator. The new designators begin with an "M" for the US Army, the "M" followed by Arabic numerals. The numerals at one time indicated the original year of adoption, such as the M1917 machine gun being first standardized in 1917. The numerals now indicate when the device was adopted in relationship to other pieces of equipment of the same general type, such as the M60 LMG.

As a general rule, changes in the basic model of a device have been followed by a capital "A" followed by an Arabic numeral, such as the M1919A4 and M1919A6 machine guns. There have also been added capital-letter suffixes to indicate a major adaptation of a weapon, such as the M60C and M60D. Experimental changes in issue equipment have been identified by the capital letter "E" followed by an Arabic numeral. In some cases, the E-designator remains after the weapon has been adopted, particularly for materials that are used by other services, such as the M60E3 and E4. Other services may use the Army designator for a specific weapon, or one of their own choosing, particularly if a weapon has been modified to fit a specific requirement.

For material type-classified for issue by the US Navy, equipment is given a Mark (Mk or MK) and Modification (Mod) number. For the initial issue of a piece of equipment, the Mod number is 0, such as the Mark 43 Mod 0 Machine Gun. Further modifications to the equipment result in an increase in the Mod number sequentially, such as Mark 144 Mod 1, Mark 144 Mod 2, and so forth.

weapon a clean gas system. The drawback was that it added to the weight of the barrel assembly. The barrel latch was now on an extension from the front of the T52E1 receiver. With the bolt cocked, the barrel latch was lifted to release the barrel assembly and the barrel drawn forward off the weapon. This method of barrel change was extremely fast and remained with the design for the rest of the series.

Additional barrels were made for the T52E1 including a light (4.5lb) and heavy (7lb) version. Several T52E1 specimens were produced and tested, but the gun would not function in one of the tests and was withdrawn. Later examination suggested that the link used and possible dust intrusion prevented the weapon from operating properly. This failure resulted in additional changes to improve the performance of the design. The T52E2, produced by May 1950, went back to the gas-impingement system of operation to try to increase the power available to cycle the weapon. In spite of the improvements, the direct connection to the original FG 42 remained – the trigger housing was still that of the German weapon. The stock, pistol grip, and fore grip of the T52E2 were of machined wood, as had been those same parts on the FG 42 Ausf. G.

The T161 series

By 1950, the War Department Equipment Board had revised and finalized the recommendations of those boards that preceded it. At the end of December 1950, the findings of the board were published in the new Army Equipment Development Guide, which was intended to direct further American weapons development. One of the recommendations of the Equipment Board was that a new .30-cal cartridge be developed for use in rifles and machine guns. That round was the T65, development of which had begun in 1945. Another recommendation was for the development of a new LMG, one that would be rugged, accurate, reliable, and simple to operate. Neither the new machine gun nor its mounts were to add more than 25lb to the standard load of an infantryman. The gun would replace the M1919A4 and M1919A6 .30-cal LMGs as well as the M1917A1 .30-cal HMG. It had to have a maximum weight of 18lb, a disintegrating belt feed, a cyclic rate of about 600rpm, a quick-change barrel with a fixed headspace, and a flash hider.

The T161E1 machine gun fitted with a heavy barrel. This was the first weapon of the T161 series to be completed for use with the T65 cartridge. It was based on all of the best characteristics of the T52 series with the design intended for mass production. No parts of the weapon are made of wood, with the forearm, pistol grip, butt stock, and the top of the feed cover made of or covered with flexible synthetic rubber. (US Government)

To accelerate the program, and ensure that a satisfactory weapon would be developed, in April 1951 a second contract was let for another design, the contract going to the Inland Manufacturing Division of the General Motors Corporation (GMC) in Dayton, Ohio. The new weapon was the T161 .30-cal gun and it was to be modeled after the T52. One particular specification for the T161 was that it be chambered for the standard .30 M2 round, meaning that a weapon would be available in case the T65 round was not adopted into service. Yet before the first T161 was ready for the engineering tests, the .30 M2 requirement was abandoned. All of the T161 series would be chambered for the T65 round, the first weapons feeding with the T55 link belts.

For the T161, particular attention was placed on making the weapon easy to mass produce. A complete design study of the T52 series was conducted to correct obvious weaknesses, simplify manufacturing, and add new features. The best features of the T52 series that had so far been produced were adopted into the T161. The basic weapon was intended to be fired from the shoulder, hip, or prone position, and provision was made for an integral bipod on the barrel as well as for attaching the weapon to a tripod mount. The stock was cushioned and in direct line with the bore and recoiling parts of the action. This in-line aspect helped minimize the forces of recoil moving the weapon off the target as it was fired.

Inland Manufacturing designed both a light and heavy barrel for the T161. The heavy barrel was covered in aluminum for better cooling and lighter construction. The increased heat conductivity of the aluminum helped draw the heat from the steel barrel, and the greater surface area made by adding the aluminum improved the barrel's heat-radiating ability. This system was a simplified version of the aluminum cooling system used on the Lewis gun. The T161 also used an improved gas-expansion system for operation.

Molded synthetic materials were used to cover the metal hand guard and barrel cover as well as the trigger housing, cheek pad, and butt stock. Developed specifically for use with the T161 series, the synthetic material had a surface consistency much like rubber, but was resistant to heat, cold, oils, acids, and alkalis. This made it a much better material for application to the T161 than wood or other plastics.

The stock assembly now had a hinged shoulder rest, which the operator could use to hold the weapon more firmly in place when firing from the prone position. The feed mechanism was simplified so that it could be disassembled quickly for cleaning, repair, or replacement with a minimum of tools. An improved rear sight was added to the package. Throughout the gun, friction was minimized by using roller bearings at all friction points. The use of roller bearings was particularly important at the point where the bolt and operating rod fitted together, as well as where a lug on the bolt operated the belt-feed mechanism. New on the T161, the lug that operated the belt feed had been moved from the operating rod to the rear of the bolt body. Additional changes and redesigns of some of the parts helped the T161 design better to absorb and utilize the forces of friction and recoil as well as vibration.

No tools were necessary to strip the T161 design for cleaning. Simple tools were needed to take apart the gas system or remove the flash hider and bipod. Two of the new weapons were assembled and test fired in December 1951. Cracks developed in several of the parts and they were replaced and the system upgraded. An additional 11 T161 weapons were produced and delivered for testing.

Simultaneous development of the T52 and T161

Early in 1953, the best features of the T52, T52E1, and T52E2 were combined into a single weapon, the T52E3. After engineering tests at Aberdeen Proving Ground, ten guns were sent to the Army for field tests in March 1953. Here was the first of the real users' tests of the new LMG concept, and the feedback would be used to continue the development of the T52 series. To mount the weapon, the T178 tripod was developed. The T178 series of tripod mounts was intended to replace all of the earlier mounts used with the Browning guns with a single lightweight model. Made of aluminum, the T178 could be adjusted in height and could make fine adjustment of the machine gun's elevation, as necessary for long-range suppressive fire. Mounted on the T178, the T52E3 gun could be used as an HMG for extended periods of firing, thanks to its quick-change barrel. although the gun also had a built-in bipod as a more mobile mount.

The T52E3 had gone back to the gas-expansion system, with a longer power stroke than the E1 model. Both light and heavy barrels were developed for the T52E3, but the light barrel was not considered as effective as the heavy barrel, which could fire for longer periods of time before it needed to be changed. A new aspect of both the light and heavy barrels was that the rear of the barrel was now fitted with a Stellite insert and the bore was chrome plated at the muzzle. Stellite is a proprietary alloy containing chromium and cobalt, along with other materials. The alloy is extremely hard and wear-resistant, even at very high temperatures. It is very difficult to machine, however, so parts made from Stellite are usually precision-cast. Making part of the chamber and barrel from Stellite

The T52E3 fitted with a heavy barrel. The rear sight of the weapon, visible above the front of the feed cover, has been directly derived from that of the original FG 42. (US Government)

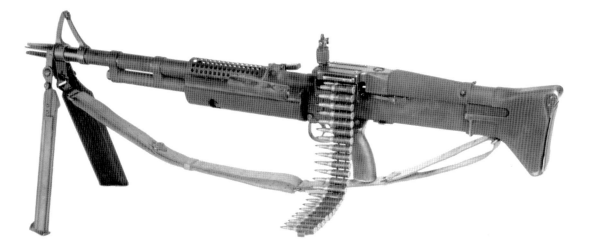

The T52E3 fitted with the light barrel. The front sling swivel idea was quickly dropped from the design since it prevents the barrel from being completely released from the weapon. The barrel-release lever is on the top of the front of the receiver, visible at the base of the carrying handle. (US Government)

puts the alloy at the point in the barrel where the greatest damage takes place from firing. The front of the chamber, just before the rifling in the bore begins, is called the "throat" of the barrel. This is the point that is exposed to the greatest amount of heat and abrasion from the propellant gases. When the steel of a barrel gets hot, it also softens. The throat of a steel barrel will get soft enough that the base material washes away, leaving a gap the bullet has to jump to reach the rifling. This "throat washing" destroys much of the accuracy of a gun barrel; Stellite resists the wearing effect and keeps the barrel in good condition for an extended time. The chrome plating of the bore, particularly near the muzzle, also serves to protect a vulnerable portion of the barrel, and keeps the barrel accurate for longer than a bare steel barrel. Chrome also resists corrosion from the primer salts or combustion byproducts of the ammunition being fired.

The barrels of the T52E3 could be changed quickly, and resisted damage from the heat of firing, making them superior to earlier machine-gun barrels. The basic design of the T52E3 also kept the weapon light (23.5lb with the heavy barrel) because of the stamped metal used to make the receiver. The .30-cal Browning machine guns were made from machined steel riveted together; the walls of the receivers were plates of steel nearly 0.188in thick. The stamped metal receiver of the T52 series was only 0.040in thick. Besides making the new machine guns lighter, the sheet-metal design also meant they were less expensive to produce. The ballistics of the new T65 ammunition achieved a close match to that of the .30 M2 round, also in a lighter package.

A drawback with the T52E3 was that it had a good deal more parts than the standard weapons. It also required more tools for basic maintenance, and disassembly and assembly were harder to perform than with the standard weapons. The user tests of the T52E3 were completed in the summer of 1953 and the results used to develop the T52E4 design.

By this time the T161 had been developed further in parallel to the T52 series. There was a duplication of effort, but one that helped ensure that there would be a new LMG for the military as soon as practical. The T161E1 had been built by early 1952 and had all of the new characteristics and parts from the original weapon, while being chambered from the start for the new T65 round. Firing tests conducted with the T161E1 revealed some difficulties with the feeding mechanism. The feed cover and its components were reworked and modified, and those parts incorporated into the T161E2. A new short-stroke-piston gas system, still using the gas-expansion system, was also included in the T161E2 design and helped reduce the overall weight of the gun by 1lb.

In January 1953, the first of the new T161E2 weapons was tested extensively by the Inland Manufacturing Co. The weapon fired 2,000 rounds during tests by the manufacturer and an additional 350 rounds at an Army facility. With the initial testing showing that the belt-feed problem had been addressed, an additional 18 weapons were made. A 4,000-round firing test under high temperature (100° Fahrenheit) as well as high humidity (95 percent) conditions demonstrated an improved functioning of the weapon. The tests demonstrated that the new gas system was not only satisfactory but that the design could be expected to have an extended service life. The aluminum cladding on the barrel assembly of the T161E1 tended to melt under the heat of use. This problem was solved by simply eliminating the bonderized aluminum from the barrels.

Now there was a direct practical comparison conducted between the T161 series and the T52 series. The T65E5 round had been adopted by NATO as the 7.62mm NATO round with a 51mm-long cartridge case (7.62×51mm) in 1954. The bet that the new US LMG would be chambered for the T65 cartridge had been won by the designers of the new weapons. In January 1955, three of the T161E2 weapons and two of the T53E4 models, along with spare parts, belted 7.62mm NATO ammunition assembled with the T55 link, and two each of the T178E1 and T182 tripod mounts were sent out for Arctic testing.

The cold-weather testing included firing at -65° Fahrenheit with the weapons both lubricated and dry – an ordeal that really hammers a weapon and brings out any weaknesses in the design. The T161E2 design completed the Arctic tests with a generally satisfactory rating. The T52E4 did not meet the demands of the testing, primarily because of a flaw in the feed system. The roller cam parts of the belt feed suffered the most failures, the components constantly breaking in the severe cold weather. Testers found that the location of the lug on the operating rod of the T52 design, as compared to placement on the bolt of the T161, put excessive stress on the belt-feed system. The location of that roller-bearing lug, which was necessary to transfer motion from the operating rod to the belt feed, was one of the major design differences between the T161 and the T52 series.

Both weapons underwent study in an attempt to improve them. The focus on the T161E2 was on increasing the component life and improving functionality, particularly in the dust test. One of the T161E2 models underwent a 25,000-round firing test using only two barrels. The sustained-fire rate for the weapon was 100rpm with a barrel change every 10 minutes. During the firing test, that single T161E2 kept firing for over four hours. The weapon showed that the system of switching between barrels as one heated up from firing could be maintained for an extended time.

The T65 cartridge

In March 1944, a memo was put forward by the US Office of the Chief of Ordnance to explore the possibility of the commercial .300-cal Savage cartridge case being loaded with military projectiles. This low-priority project was the beginning of what would be the development of the T65 round. This idea had first been fielded by the German military in 1943 with the MP 43/StG 44 assault rifle. This carbine-sized weapon could shoot on both semi-automatic and full-automatic, but fired an "intermediate" cartridge (*Mittelpatrone*), the 7.92×33mm *kurz* ("short"), that was mid-sized between a pistol round such as the German 9×19mm Parabellum ammunition, and the standard German 7.92×57mm rifle round. The cartridge was intended to have a maximum effective range[1] of about 400yd, as compared to the 1,000yd-plus range of the standard rifle round. The average infantry engagement took place at less than 400yd, so the additional range capability of the full-sized round was mostly wasted. A smaller cartridge would have correspondingly less recoil and be more controllable on full-automatic fire. Additionally, it would require less in the way of strategic war materials to make.

In the postwar years, a number of countries sought similar "intermediate" rounds of ammunition for selective-fire infantry rifles. In the United States, though, the ideal was for a "full-power" military .30-cal cartridge in a shorter, lighter case and with an effective range of nearly 900yd. The intention was that the round would be issued for a new family of weapons that would replace the standard M1 Garand rifle and the issue machine guns (M1917A1, M1919A4, and M1919A6) with the M14 rifle and the M60 LMG.

The first of the T65 rounds were made in 1945 to be used in select-fire conversions of the M1 Garand rifle. The rounds were standard military .30-cal ball bullets loaded into cases that were nearly identical to those of the commercial .300 Savage. The case for those first rounds was 1.97in (49.5mm) long. The T65E1 round used

ABOVE Left to right: 7.62×51mm (7.62 NATO) M59 Ball; 7.92×57mm (8mm Mauser) Tracer; 7.62×63mm (30-06) M1 Ball.

the same length cartridge case with a different bullet and propellant charge. The final cartridge in the series was the T65E5 round with the FAT1E3 case that was 2.01in (51mm) long.

In spite of European and other US allies desiring a lighter round that fired a smaller bullet, the US military pushed for the adoption of the new .30-cal round. NATO finally folded in the face of the pressure from the United States and formally adopted the 7.62×51mm cartridge as the basic NATO round in 1954. This meant that in times of conflict, all members of NATO could be supplied with standardized ammunition from their allies.

In the US military, the definition for effective range of a firearm is the distance that an average soldier can be expected to hit a man-sized target 50 percent of the time.

In spite of its performance, there were still flaws in the T161E2 that prevented it being considered as a replacement for the Browning M1917A1, M1919A4, and M1919A6 guns. The gas system was considered unreliable because of carbon buildup, which caused malfunctions and a complete failure of the gun to operate. Additionally, the firing pin was susceptible to breakage. A broken firing pin could result in the weapon firing out of battery (when the weapon fires before the bolt is properly locked to the barrel). The front rollers of the operating rod also proved susceptible to breaking, a major flaw in the weapon. The new rear sight had no proper adjustment for windage and the front sight bent too easily. It was also at this time that the testing board recommended that the lightweight (3lb) barrel be dropped. So in spite of the weapon being

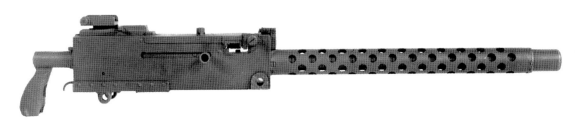

considered very successful, several of the components were improved and their new design incorporated into the T161E3. During the second half of 1955, 20 of the original T161E2 weapons were converted over to the E3 configuration and 100 of the new T161E3 design were manufactured.

All of the efforts for the T52 series became concentrated in the development of the T52E5 design. The Bridge Tool & Die Works received a contract for the development and construction of a T52E5 design that would incorporate all of the best characteristics of the previous versions. Additionally, the new weapon would include some of the design characteristics of the T161E2 and utilize a new link design. The T55 link created a heavy inflexible belt that was harder for the feed system to draw into the weapon. A lighter and more flexible belt would feed more positively, with less strain on the belt and the gun, decreasing the amount of belt-pulling power that had to be supplied by the belt-feed and gas system of the weapon. The new link was the T89, made from stamped, formed sheet metal. The link was lighter in construction than the T55, but held the round more securely due to a detent tab on an extension from the body of the link. The tab clipped into the extractor groove of a cartridge case, holding the round firmly. Like all of the other links in the series, the T89 was a disintegrating type. After the round had been stripped out of the belt, the link that had been holding it separated from the rest of the ammunition and could be ejected away from the gun. This system prevented an expended belt from dangling from the weapon and possibly entangling the gunner while he was on the move. The

The air-cooled Browning M1919A4 light machine gun. Though it could be hand-held and fired, this weapon was normally mounted on an M2 tripod for general use. Derived directly from the water-cooled M1917, versions of this weapon served all over the world with US forces and their allies. During World War II, it was normally loaded with a 250-round fabric belt. Later in that war and during Korea and into Vietnam, the M1919A4 was loaded with a metallic ammunition belt made of disintegrating links. (Author)

An Army manual photo of the Browning M1919A4 light machine gun mounted on the M2 tripod. The traverse and elevating mechanism can be seen underneath the rear of the weapon. The T&E gear allows for fine adjustment of the weapon when firing, or aiming along pre-selected lines of defense when firing in the dark. (US Army)

The T161E3, the final design of the series, this specimen fitted with a 100-round sheet-metal ammunition can. The ribbed strip extending out the right side of the weapon is attached to the end of the ammunition belt and is used as an aid to loading. The can was considered too heavy and noisy to use on a combat weapon. The front sight of this T161E3 specimen is fitted with an adjustable front sight post that would allow the barrel to have been zeroed to the weapon, rather than having to change the rear sight adjustment each time the barrel was changed. That adjustable front sight post was eliminated before the T161E3 was adopted as the M60 light machine gun. (US Government)

new T89 link also caused changes in the T161E3 design, since the belt-feed system had to be modified to operate with the new ammunition belts.

Testing in late 1955 at Aberdeen Proving Ground indicated that the T161E3 was superior in endurance to the earlier weapons. It also operated better in dusty and rainy conditions than the other weapons. The gun was not as accurate as the M1917A1 when set up on a tripod, but weighting the legs of the T178 tripod increased the accuracy of sustained fire, giving the T161E3 comparable performance to that of the water-cooled Browning. Aberdeen Proving Ground recommended modifications to the T178 tripod and that the new tripod mount be submitted for user tests.

Throughout the testing phase, the control weapons that the T52 and T161 series had to compete against were the Browning designs already in use with the military. By the spring of 1956, reports on the testing of the T161E3, including a new series of Arctic trials, stated that the T161E3 gun and its mount had a number of advantages over the standard .30-cal guns and their mounts. Notably, the T161E3 could be stripped down and assembled again in about half the time of the control weapons, and could be handled more easily by the gunners, whether wearing mittens or firing the gun from the bipod. The T161E3 could also be fired from the hip and shoulder position. The gunners considered the new gun lighter, shorter, and easier to maintain. They liked it.

A modified version of the T178 tripod, the T178E2, had been brought into testing with the T161E3. The new tripod mount had some differences in the location of the controls and had been made simpler to operate when wearing gloves. The T178E2 weighed about 25lb; it could be adjusted for height and used for indirect fire.

The military testing board found that the T161E3 was superior to the M1917A1, M1919A4, and M1919A6 machine guns in simplicity, portability, reliability under adverse conditions, ease of maintenance, and application of fire. One problem found during the testing was that sections of the new weapon were difficult to clean. This cleaning difficulty was traced to the excessive fouling from the new M59 7.62mm NATO ball round that was used during the tests. Additional accessories were developed and tested with the T161E3, including a spare barrel bag that could hold an extra barrel, an asbestos mitten (used to change a hot barrel), and maintenance tools and supplies.

The M60

In February 1957, the T161E3 design was standardized as the new M60 machine gun, and the Browning .30-cal weapons were designated as limited standard. The T178E2 tripod was standardized as the M91 and the T89 belt link became the M13 metallic belt cartridge link.

The new M60 with its integral bipod weighed about 8lb less than the M1919A4 gun without a mount and 18lb less than the water-cooled M1917A1. Unlike the earlier weapons, the M60 could be used effectively for assault-type actions, being fired from the shoulder, under-arm, or hip with relative ease. The slow cyclic rate of fire of the M60, about 600rpm, was not considered a handicap, as it meant that a good gunner could easily fire short bursts or even single shots accurately by just manipulating the trigger. No headspace adjustment, something that had to be done with all of the Browning machine-gun designs, was necessary with the M60.

Ammunition for the M60 came in 100-round belts, each belt packaged in a chipboard box. The ammunition belts for general combat use were made up of repeating orders of four rounds of ball ammunition followed by a round of tracer ammunition, the individual rounds held together by M13 metal links. The box was itself carried in a simple cloth bag with a long shoulder strap that could be slung from the shoulder and carried as the T4 bandoleer. A bracket on the left side of the M60's receiver could receive a canvas-and-metal magazine. Ripping the top off the chipboard ammunition box and putting it in the canvas magazine gave a stable source of ammunition for assault fire. The M60 could also be fired from longer belts held in M1A1 (275-round), M19A1 (200-round) or larger metal ammunition cans when shooting from the bipod or tripod.

A machine-gun crew demonstrates the newly adopted M60 light machine gun in May 1958. The men are members of the United States Army Infantry School at Fort Benning, Georgia. The weapon is mounted on the M91 tripod and the assistant gunner is feeding the belt into the side of the weapon for firing. (NARA)

Operating the M60

To load and fire the M60 the bolt has to be drawn back to the cocked position. To cock the gun, the safety lever on the left side of the pistol grip needs to be in the FIRE (up) position. With the safety on FIRE, the cocking handle on the right side of the receiver is drawn back until the bolt is held to the rear by the trigger mechanism. With the bolt locked to the rear, the cocking handle is pushed to the fully forward position where a spring detent holds it in place. The safety is now pushed into the SAFE (down) position.

With the weapon cocked the feed cover is opened by twisting the feed-cover latch on the right side of the receiver at the upper rear. The feed cover is lifted up and then the feed tray, which is hinged at the front as well, is lifted. With the breech of the M60 exposed, the gunner looks to see that the way is clear and the chamber empty.

The end of an ammunition belt is removed from the container. This container can be: (1) a chipboard box and bandoleer placed in the canvas magazine attached to the receiver of an early M60; (2) the chipboard box held in the bandoleer with the cloth bandoleer slipped over the hanger attached to the feed tray; (3) a larger container such as an ammunition box on a mounting system. Whatever method is used to supply ammunition, the feed is in from the left side of the weapon and, with the

In late August 1969, as part of a long-range patrol, this patrol leader opens fire on the enemy with his M60 machine gun. The orange tips of the tracers in his ammunition belt can be seen in the picture. The tracers are spaced out with four rounds of ball ammunition between each tracer. (NARA)

THE M60 EXPOSED

Machine Gun, Caliber 7.62mm, M60

1 Flash suppressor
2 Bipod
3 Gas vent
4 Gas-cylinder extension
5 Gas-port plug
6 Gas piston
7 Gas cylinder
8 Gas-cylinder nut
9 Gas tube
10 Operating-rod drive spring
11 Operating rod
12 Operating-rod yoke
13 Trigger pin
14 Trigger
15 Trigger spring
16 Sear
17 Sear spring
18 Pistol grip
19 Sear notch
20 Safety lever
21 Operating-rod drive-spring guide
22 Buffer plunger
23 Buffer spring
24 Hinged shoulder rest
25 Butt stock
26 Buffer locking plate
27 Feed cover
28 Bolt plug
29 Actuating cam roller
30 Firing-pin spring
31 Bolt
32 Cover pin
33 Firing pin
34 Rear sight
35 Locking lugs
36 Breech
37 Barrel-locking lever
38 Carrying handle
39 Forearm assembly
40 Barrel
41 Gas port
42 Front sight

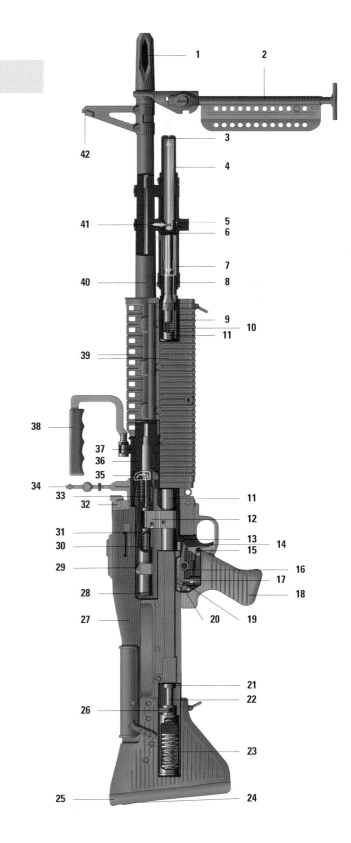

open side of the links facing down, the first round in the belt is placed in the open groove on the feed tray. If there is a link exposed on the end of the belt, it is slipped into the link-ejection guide on the right side of the feed tray. The belt is held in place while the feed cover is pushed down and locked in place. The safety lever is pushed up to fire and the trigger pulled. The M60 will continue to fire as long as the trigger is held back and there is ammunition in the feed tray.

When the trigger is pulled, the sear at the top of the trigger mechanism releases the operating rod, which is driven forward from the pressure of the compressed operating-rod spring. The forward lug on the bolt has a small extension that strikes the base of the cartridge in the groove of the feed tray, pushing it forward. As the bolt moves forward to strip the round into the chamber, the actuating cam roller bearing at the rear of the bolt moves through the long angled feed cam that runs more than half the length of the feed cover. The feed cam is moved to the side as the actuating cam roller moves down the channel running the length of the part. The movement of the front of the feed cam is reversed by the feed cam lever pivoting on its support stud; the opposite end of the feed cam lever moves the pawl carrier assembly to the left. The spring-loaded feed pawls move over the next round in the belt and snap down on the left side of the cartridge.

The nose of the cartridge being stripped forward by the bolt strikes the chambering ramp in the receiver and is moved down and forward toward the barrel socket. The bolt continues to move forward, pushing the cartridge down the feed ramp, into the barrel socket and into the chamber of the barrel itself. The face of the bolt enters the barrel socket, pushing the cartridge ahead of it. When the cartridge is fully seated in the chamber, the extractor on the bolt snaps over the head of the case and locks into the extractor groove on the cartridge. The ejector pin and spring on the left side of the bolt face is compressed after the cartridge as the cartridge moves fully into the chamber.

When the round is fully forward, the bolt has entered the barrel socket to its maximum depth. After the bolt has come to its fully forward position, the operating rod continues to move forward independently of the bolt. The operating-rod lug that extends up from the rod and into the bolt body now acts on the cam slot in the bolt. As the operating-rod lug moves through the cam slot, it rotates the bolt a quarter-turn clockwise. As the bolt rotates, the locking lugs on the top and bottom of the bolt head enter the locking recesses in the barrel socket. Once the lugs have been fully seated in their rotation, the bolt is locked to the barrel and ceases any movement.

The operating rod continues moving forward, the lug passing through a straight portion of the cam slot on the bolt body. The upper part of the operating-rod lug has a U-shaped channel that fits over the firing pin held in the bolt body. Two spools on the firing pin hold it in place in the operating-rod lug and the firing pin is moved forward as the operating rod moves. The front of the firing pin crushes the percussion cap in the base of the cartridge, firing the chambered round.

As the bullet moves down the barrel, part of the propellant gas is tapped off through the gas port. The gas enters the gas cylinder through the port and into the hollow gas piston through the ports around its head. Once the gas has reached enough pressure, the piston moves to the rear. The ports on the piston body move out of line with the gas port and more propellant gases are prevented from entering the cylinder. The solid head at the back of the gas piston presses on the front surface of the operating rod, forcing it back. Once the piston has reached the end of its rearward travel, the gas port is open and excess gases escape through the bleeder hole at the front of the gas-cylinder extension under the front of the barrel.

The rearward movement of the operating rod pushes the lug backward in the cam slot of the bolt. The lug forces the bolt to rotate a quarter-turn counter-clockwise, moving the locking lugs out of the locking recesses in the barrel socket. The length of the cam slot helps ensure that the bolt will not rotate and unlock until the gas pressure in the barrel has dropped to a safe level. Once the bolt is unlocked, it continues to move to the rear from the action of the operating rod. The fired cartridge is pulled from the chamber by the extractor. As the bolt moves to the rear, the actuating cam roller at the rear of the bolt moves back through the channel in the feed cam, forcing it to move. The direction of travel of the feed cam now moves the carrier pawl assembly to the right, moving the round held by the belt-feed pawls into the groove in the feed tray.

In May 1958, a machine-gun crew operates an M60 at the US Army Infantry School at Fort Benning, Georgia, very soon after the weapon was adopted. The assistant gunner is carefully feeding the belt from an ammunition can into the feed tray of the weapon. On the left shoulder of the assistant gunner can be seen the "Follow Me" patch as worn by men of the US Army Infantry Center and Infantry School. (NARA)

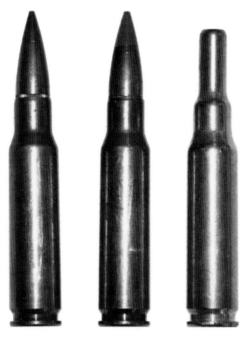

Left to right: M59 Ball, M62 Tracer, and M82 Blank. These three 7.62×51mm rounds are the three standard combat rounds for the 1960s and were the only rounds listed in a number of the manuals.

Once the bolt has moved back far enough, the ejector pin and spring push on the back of the fired cartridge case, tossing it out of the weapon through the ejection slot in the right side of the receiver. At the same time, the pressure of the new round moving into place on the feed tray forces the empty belt link out of the right side of the feed cover through a small ejection port. When the operating rod reaches the rear of its travel, the operating-rod spring is fully compressed. Excess energy from the movement of the bolt to the rear is absorbed and softened by the buffer assembly.

If the trigger remains pulled, the operating-rod spring pushes the operating rod forward, beginning another cycle of firing. If the trigger is held back after the last shot has been fired, the bolt slams forward and locks against the empty breech. The bolt remains forward until the cocking handle is pulled back. If the feed cover is opened, it cannot be closed properly unless the bolt is fully rearward in the cocked position, so that the actuating cam roller on the back of the bolt can properly enter the channel in the feed cam. If the feed cover is closed with the bolt in the forward position, the bolt will jam and cannot be drawn back by the cocking lever until the feed cover is opened.

A left-side view of an early-production M60 machine gun. The bracket to secure a magazine assembly is riveted to the receiver directly underneath the opening to the feed tray. The rear sight is in the folded (down) position for traveling. (Author)

USE
Portable firepower

Until the arrival of the M60, the US military had not had a light belt-fed machine gun in its inventory. In general, an LMG is a machine gun that fires a round no larger than rifle caliber and is of a size that it can be carried and employed by one man. MMGs and HMGs are usually mounted on a form of tripod and are capable of long periods of sustained fire. The LMG accompanies the infantry and is their major source of individual fire. The medium and heavy machine guns support the infantry by supplying cover and suppressing the enemy at the objective the infantry is approaching.

By World War II, all sides in the conflict recognized the value of an LMG to augment the firepower of the troops in rapidly moving warfare. The Germans had their very fine MG 34 and (from 1942) MG 42 machine guns, and based their tactics on one of those weapons being available at the squad level. The Americans used the BAR as a base of fire for the squad. One of the tactical applications was that the squad automatic riflemen (armed with the BAR) would use the firepower of their weapon to help cover the less mobile medium and heavy machine guns in the form of the M1919A4 and M1917A1 weapons respectively.

The M1917A1 remained in wide use in the US military, but it was the same heavy weapon that it had been in World War I – man-portable, but only in sections, and unsuited to rapid squad maneuvers or the quick acquisition of a sudden target. The M1919A4 and M1919A6 could be hip-fired by a strong operator, but only when being fed by a short section of belt. Many LMG machine-gunners, particularly in the Pacific theater, would carry their weapons on an improvised sling across the shoulder and chest, with a 20–30-round section of ammunition belt dangling down from the left side of the gun. This arrangement allowed a machine gun to be brought to bear quickly on a target such as a sniper in a tree or an enemy soldier popping up from a hidden foxhole. Soldiers made do with what they had available to them, but often via an improvised solution to a local problem. The adoption of the M60 in 1957 changed all of that, giving the US Army an effective, belt-fed machine gun that could be used on the assault, move with a squad, and still provide support fire.

INTO PRODUCTION – TESTING AND IMPROVEMENTS

Even though it was designed for mass production, the new M60 didn't reach significant output for several years following its adoption. The United States was in a time of peace and a number of new small arms – the M14 rifle and the M79 grenade launcher, among others – were competing with the M60 for budget dollars. The pilot production lines for the new M60 were set up at Springfield Armory in Massachusetts. The first M60 came off the production lines to extensive media coverage on December 29, 1958. The Armory agreed to deliver the first ten weapons and mounts in December 1958, with production gradually ramping up to meet a demand of 500 weapons per month carrying through September 1959. The Armory Operations Division completed weapons and mounts, but did not meet the production schedule.

Some of the first batches of M60s and mounts went to the US Marine Corps (USMC) and to the 101st Airborne Division at Fort Campbell, Kentucky, for user testing. Heavy wear appeared in a number of the parts during testing by the 101st Airborne, and they were replaced. These parts included the operating rod, sear, bolt, and drive spring, among others. While examining and replacing parts, developers also gave attention to the other pieces that supported the M60. New styles of canvas magazines

At Fort Devens, Massachusetts, in August 1958, Mr Jim Murphy, an R&D Gunner from Springfield Armory, demonstrates the ease of handling the new M60 machine gun. Holding the weapon over his head, Mr Murphy graphically shows how much more easily held the new lightweight weapon is over the earlier models used by the US Army. (NARA)

were designed to fit the 100-round chipboard boxes and bandoleers. A carrying bag for the spare barrel and equipment was also designed, fabricated, and tested. Designated the Spare Barrel Case, the waterproofed bag held a spare barrel and asbestos mitten in its main compartment and a combination tool, ruptured cartridge case extractor, and cleaning rod, brushes, patches, and lubricant in its outer pockets. The M91 tripod also came under re-examination. New parts were manufactured for the tripod and troop testing continued, as did demonstration firings.

Starting at Fort Benning, Georgia, 12 of the guns and mounts were used to show the capabilities of the new M60. During that same period nearly 70 weapon demonstrations took place in the United States and Europe. Allied military and political leaders were shown the features of the M60 and fired the weapons extensively. The demonstration guns burned through more than 60,000 rounds of ammunition each. More than just a series of demonstrations, the tests also established that the new guns could stand up to sustained fire.

The US airborne troops particularly liked the new weapons, and were impressed by some of what they could do. For the first time, the airborne troops of the 101st could jump with machine-gunners actually carrying their primary weapon. In this configuration, the M60 could be cocked and the barrel removed with the quick-release lever on the upper right side of the gun. The bolt would have to stay in the cocked position during the jump, a situation easily ensured by wrapping rigger's tape around the receiver of the weapon, holding the cocking lever to the rear. Both the strapped receiver and the barrel of the M60 could be packed into a padded drop bag. The paratrooper secured the drop bag on his person and continued with the drop. Once on the ground, the machine-gunner would only have to open up his drop bag, strip the rigger's tape from the receiver, lock the barrel in place, and load a belt of ammunition. The M60 would now be ready to defend a drop zone.

The airborne forces were not the only ones interested in taking the M60 into the air, though. Army aviation had been using helicopters in increasing numbers since introducing them actively in the Korean War (1950–53). They voiced an interest in adapting the new M60 to the H13 Sioux, H21 Shawnee "Flying Banana," and H34 Choctaw helicopters. There was already a weapon system in place for the H13: a pair of M37 .30-cal machine guns (a Browning M1919 variation) known collectively as the XM1 armament system. A study began into the possibilities of a helicopter-mounted M60, including weapon modifications for remote firing, remote charging, and positive safety. A preliminary mount for four weapons was to be ready for the UH-1A helicopter in March 1959.

Development of the M60 continued as endurance tests uncovered problems. A difficulty with the new M91 tripod was that it did not meet the accuracy of the older M1917A1 weapon unless the legs of the mount

A left-side view of the M60 light machine gun mounted on an M91 tripod. The legs of the tripod can be adjusted to raise or lower the height of the weapon. The tall tripod arrangement allows the weapon to be used for accurate indirect fire, firing at long range where the target cannot be seen by the gunner. This is possible in part because of the precise controls in the mount cradle at the top of the tripod which set the angle and direction of the weapon. This very early specimen of the M60 has neither the magazine bracket on the left side of the receiver, nor the bandoleer hanger under the feed tray, to hold an ammunition belt. For firing, this weapon would be fed from a long belt held in an ammunition can sitting on the ground and guided by the assistant gunner. (US Government)

In 1963, a machine-gunner with the 57th Light Helicopter Transport Co. is on his H-21 Shawnee helicopter. Helicopter armament was still in its infancy and crewmembers would often improvise their own weapons system. This gunner has attached a 250-round ammunition can to the top of an M1919A6 light machine gun, adding considerably to the 31lb weight of the weapon. There is a feed chute leading from the can into the side of the weapon and he has tied a "John Wayne" sling around the pistol grip and barrel of the machine gun. He is able to use the weapon through the open door of the helicopter, and if he has to bail out of a stricken bird, this gunner will still be armed. Rigged-up systems like this were a major factor in moving towards dedicated helicopter armament for the US Army. (NARA)

were sandbagged. The extra weight of the sandbags made the M91 more stable, but increased the amount of material required to use the gun. More material also meant more weight for the troops to carry, a problem the M60 had been intended to solve.

One of the intentions for the tall M91 tripod was to be able to angle the M60 up enough to conduct long-range "plunging fire," in which a large volume of bullets are dropped onto a broad area to inflict attrition and deny the enemy freedom of movement. Yet accuracy was of paramount importance, so the requirements for plunging fire and the necessary adjustable mounted height of the weapon were finally relaxed. A much simpler mount could be considered. That mount was an adaptation of the M2 tripod already used for the Browning M1919A4 and M1919A6 weapons. With adaptors that allowed the standard traverse and elevation (T&E) gear and pintle to be used, the M2 became the new M122 tripod for the M60. (The pintle is a tripod component with a cradle to hold the weapon, and a conical projection on the base to fit in the socket of a mount – tripod or otherwise.) The T&E

mechanism allows for fine adjustment of the weapon, even in the dark, when the gunner is guided by the clicks from the mechanism. The change in mounts gave a 5lb weight saving between the adjustable 24.6lb M91 and the 19.5lb M122 with T&E and pintle. The M122 was first made in the spring of 1959 along with two sets of the necessary adaptor kits. The M122 and mounting adaptors for the M60 were quickly made standard issue, and the M91 tripod was declared obsolete by 1960.

Another change to the basic M60 involved the method of attaching ammunition to the weapon. The original T4 bandoleer could not be fitted to the weapon directly. Instead it was inserted into a canvas-and-metal pouch (designated as a magazine) that snapped into the bracket on the left side of the receiver. By changing the design of the bandoleer and adding a vertical hanger to the feed tray of the M60, the bandoleer could be fitted directly to the M60, eliminating the need for the magazine. The new T7 bandoleer, reinforced and with a hanging strap wrapped on the side of the pouch, was adopted as the M4 bandoleer. The hanger became a standard attachment to the basic M60 feed tray and the magazine was eliminated with a weight saving of 1.2lb.

The Springfield Armory produced the M60 and variations of the weapon for a number of years. A contract was also issued to the Saco-Lowell Company (later known as Saco Defense) of Saco, Maine, to manufacture the M60 and variations. That company continued to produce the M60 for 40 years until the rights to manufacture the weapon were sold to US Ordnance, who put the weapon into production in March 2000.

The M60C

One of the first variants of the M60 to be produced was the M60C. To meet the requirements for helicopter armament systems, the M60 had been changed over to an electric solenoid trigger. The new remote firing system released the sear, firing the gun, when an electric current energized the electro-magnet that was the heart of the solenoid. The butt stock of the

The XM6 armament subsystem mounted in place on a UH-1B helicopter. The long silver feed chutes guide ammunition from the containers inside the helicopter cargo cabin to the two M60C guns attached to the mounting points above and below the end of the mount. The two dark mechanisms on the mount that the ends of the feed chuting are attached to is an electrical booster system. The booster helps pull the long ammunition belts from the containers inside the helicopter and pushes them out to the guns. This is called a quad machine gun system since there are two guns on each side of the helicopter. (NARA)

M60 was removed and the M60C had a simple shaped sheet-metal cover over the rear of the receiver. The forearm assembly was also removed as unnecessary on the M60C; its removal allowed passing air to aid in cooling the barrel. The new M60 variant was first produced at the Springfield Armory facilities, with delivery of the first 900 weapons completed by September 1963.

The M60C was immediately scheduled to be used in the Armament Subsystem, Helicopter, 7.62 MG: Quad, M6. Additional parts of the helicopter armament system included a remote means to charge the weapon (cock the action for firing). The ammunition feed to the machine guns was conducted through flexible chutes that were attached to the receivers of the guns. From ammunition boxes that ran nearly the width of the helicopter cargo compartment, 1,500 rounds were available to feed each M60C. The mounts for the guns were also able to be moved and aimed from the cockpit under the control of the copilot while the pilot handled flying the bird. Two of the complete mounts were attached to the sides of a Huey UH-1B helicopter. The twin M60C guns on each side of the helicopter in the M6 system were the original armament for what would become in a very short time the legendary helicopter gunship of the Vietnam War.

A close-up of the M60C as it is installed on the M6 armament system. (NARA)

The M60 Machine Gun (Modified)

Additional variations of the basic M60 were developed in the first years of the 1960s. The issue of weight was never fully satisfactory to the engineers or the users of the M60. One of the problems with the weapon was that there was an extra gas system included with each barrel. The idea had been that a fresh barrel would bring along with it a cool, and hopefully clean, gas system. The bipod of the gun was attached to the barrel assembly, not the weapon proper. When a hot barrel had to be changed, the gunner had to hold up the weapon while the assistant gunner switched barrels. The assistant gunner also had to be concerned with the heat of the barrel he was taking off the gun. If he didn't have the heavy asbestos mitten that was issued with the spare barrel, he would have to try and hold a hot barrel by the bipod leg – a clumsy arrangement at best. There was a carrying handle on the M60, but it was attached to the receiver of the weapon. The carrying handle could be used to hold the weapon up, but not to help change the barrel.

To address these and other perceived problems with the M60, from October 1962 a new modified version was designed and built at Springfield Armory. It was to be ready the following year, with 25 guns produced by July 1963. The entire order for what was called the M60 Machine Gun (Modified) was for 3,000 weapons and 100 sets of spare parts.

In the M60 (Modified) the gas system was dismounted from the barrel and permanently attached to the front of the receiver. There was a dovetail mounting bracket on top of the gas system that matched to a bracket on the bottom of the barrel, centered on the gas port. The top of the forearm assembly was cut away to clear space for the carrying handle that was moved to the barrel itself. The bipod assembly was removed from the front of the barrel and a lighter bipod developed with a mounting system that went around the gas cylinder. The piston inside of the gas cylinder was also redesigned so that it could not be put in backwards. It operated correctly no matter how the operator inserted it into the cylinder after cleaning.

The modified barrel assembly now weighed 2.25lb less than the original design. A simplified rear sight with increased windage adjustment was added and the feed cover, fore-end, and feed tray made from castings. Overall weight of the weapon dropped to an empty weight of 23.7lb in the initial specimens.

The M60 (Modified) eventually received the unofficial designation M60E1. In spite of testing over a period of years, the modified design was never adopted. Among other deficiencies, it would not operate in cold weather as well as the basic M60 design, was generally less reliable, and less accurate. The design was shelved by the end of the 1960s and never went into full production.

The M60B

There was another very limited production version of the M60 that did see combat duty. Developed in 1963, the M6 helicopter armament package

was a mounted system with the weapons on the outside of the helicopter. Firing the weapons was performed by the copilot in the front of the aircraft. For the crew of a helicopter, particularly the UH-1 Huey, a weapon was needed for the men sitting on either side of the aircraft, the door gunners.

To make a weapon easier for the door gunners to handle than the standard M60, some limited modifications were implemented to the weapon in 1965–66. The bipod was usually removed to make the weapon lighter. The rear sight was also removed and a small bracket slipped into the dovetail; the bracket allowed a carabiner ring to be attached to the top of the receiver and the weapon hung from the overhead with an elastic shock cord assembly. The butt stock was removed and replaced with a rubber boot, which the door gunner simply tucked up tightly into his armpit in the underarm firing position. Instead of using the sights, the door-gunner guided his aim by watching the track of the tracers he fired.

The modified door-gunner's weapon was referred to as the M60B model. There is no specific date available for when the variation was first produced, and the designation is an unofficial one. But the M60B was well received by the helicopter gunners who used it, and saw duty in the helicopters flying in the skies of Vietnam. Feeding the weapon from large ammunition boxes attached to the deck of the cargo compartment could be difficult, however. The door-gunner would typically move his weapon over a wide arc during a mission and the long belt could get tangled or, worse still, refuse to feed, or even break off from the feed tray of the gun. A field correction was found for this problem. The two levers that snap over the end of a feed chute on the sides of the magazine mounting plate were just wide enough to clip over the end of a B3 metal C-ration can. Slipping the can between the levers held it in place; the curved surface of the can lifted and straightened out the belt so that it fed directly and smoothly into the weapon, curing the feed problems.

The Vietnam machine gun (previous pages)

At the Battle of Ia Drang in November 1965, US forces met forces of the People's Army of (North) Vietnam in major direct combat. These heavily outnumbered men of the 1st Battalion of the 7th Cavalry Regiment are fighting thousands of enemy forces at Landing Zone X-Ray in the Ia Drang Valley in the Central Highlands of South Vietnam. All of the weapons of the American forces are being brought to bear on the enemy surrounding them on all sides. The M60 machine guns are employed here to defend the landing zone itself as a bird is coming in. The M60s are being employed in all of their configurations, tripod mounted, bipod mounted, and shoulder fired, as they pour out fire. Assistant gunners and ammunition carriers tear open cans of ammunition to keep the guns firing. Though stripped of its heavy armament in order to carry more critical supplies and extract the worst of the wounded, the incoming Huey has its door gunners also firing their M60 machine guns into the enemy forces.

The M60D

The M60B, as a door-gunner weapon, was quickly supplanted by a more purpose-built modification to the basic M60. In July 1965, a priority order was issued with a nearly impossible delivery time. The order was for 670 M60 basic guns converted to the M60D version to be used in the XM23 and XM24 helicopter armament systems.

The configuration of the M60D went back to the general outline of the .50-cal machine gun. Instead of a pistol grip under the center of the receiver and a rear stock, the M60D had a pair of vertical grips on the back of the weapon. Between the two grips were loops for the index finger of both hands. The loops connected to the sear mechanism of the M60D and acted as the triggers. Another modification was the removal of the adjustable rear sight and its replacement with a "speed-ring" type sight. The speed-ring sight is not as precise as a typical post-and-notch firearms sight, but the large ring with a central smaller ring is very fast to use, particularly against a fleeting target.

The demand for the guns was combined with a requirement for new parts to improve the operation of the weapons in Vietnam. The delivery date was the end of September that same year. Along with Saco-Lowell in Maine, the Springfield Armory worked to meet the demand, and the new guns were ready for use in Vietnam on time.

The basic M23 armament subsystem was a pintle mount, ammunition box, and feed components, and it could put an M60D along with 600 rounds of ammunition on either side of a Huey. The gun could be operated by a sitting gunner secured into his position, with feed chuting linking the ammunition box to the side of the weapon. Ammunition belts were guided up the chuting and into the side of the weapon, eliminating the need for the C-ration can modification, and making for a very secure mount. The gunner would hold the M60D by the spade grips and use the speed-ring and front sight post to aim at targets on the ground. In this mount the gun could be slung about quickly, switching from the front of the helicopter to the rear.

Right and left side views of the M60D taken in 1964. (NARA)

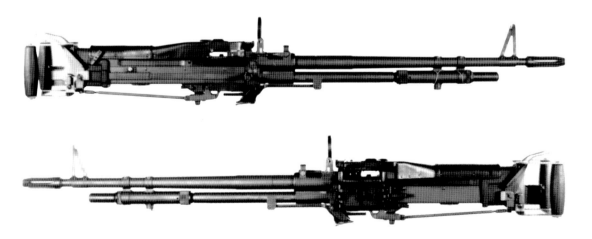

In Honduras, an American UH-1H helicopter of the 1st Cavalry Division waits with a number of Honduran soldiers aboard. The door-gunner is manning his M60D machine gun. The Hondurans are holding their weapons muzzle-down for safety while on board the helicopter. The men are taking part in a joint exercise between Honduran and American forces, Exercise *Granadero I*, in May 1984. (US Department of Defense)

In an emergency, the M60D could be dismounted and used from the bipod in a ground-defense mode. The M60D was also used in the M24 armament subsystem, which could be mounted as window guns in the larger cargo helicopters such as the CH-47 Chinook. The M24 system was smaller and only held 200 rounds for the single M60D it mounted. A large canvas bag was often mounted on the right side of the M60D guns in both the M23 and M24 systems in order to secure ejected brass and links. The bags helped prevent empty brass or links from causing any damage to the interior of the helicopters.

INTO VIETNAM

Helicopter use

As US forces began direct combat operations in Vietnam in the spring of 1965, the M60 machine gun was one of the first weapons on the ground. On the morning of March 8, 1965, at Da Nang in South Vietnam, the first of 3,500 Marines began landing. The soldiers were armed with the new weapons designed for the military in the 1950s – the M14 rifle and the M60 machine gun. It did not take long for them to try out their weapons in direct combat. When the Viet Cong attacked the Da Nang Airbase on July 1, 1965, the Marines and Air Force personnel fought back hard. For the first time, the Vietnamese communists heard the thunder of the M60s directed against them.

Shortly after the first Marines stepped onto Vietnam's shores, Army troops also began arriving in large numbers in Vietnam. In 1965, some of these troops belonged to a new concept in Army operations: Airmobile (or AirCav) – cavalry troops who rode helicopters into battle rather than horses. These troops were armed with the new 5.56mm M16 rifle, and the M60 machine gun.

The helicopter proved invaluable in Vietnam for moving masses of troops quickly. With aerial movement, men and material went over, instead of through, the jungle to an objective. The B model of the Huey helicopter could carry only eight fully loaded combat troops. The C model could carry the same number of troops, but had a more stable blade system and made a better gun platform. The Huey D model could carry 12 troops, or a large assortment of weapons and ammunition.

By March 1965, the original M6 armament system had been upgraded with the addition of 2.75in rocket pods. Each side of a Huey gunship equipped with the new M16 armament system now had two M60C forward-firing guns, an M60-armed door gunner, and a seven-round M158 rocket pod suspended from the same mount that held the fixed machine guns. The copilot still handled aiming and firing the M60C machine guns, but it was the pilot, by aligning the helicopter, who aimed and fired the 2.75in rockets. The rockets could be fitted with a variety of warheads and fired effectively out to a range of 1,600yd.

The age of the helicopter gunship had begun. The Huey gunship version had an M16 armament system fitted along with a pair of door guns; there would be a wide assortment of other weapons on board the helicopter for use by the crew in flight, and if they had to abandon the aircraft in enemy territory. The other common helicopter arrangement was the troop carrier or "slick." The nickname came from the troop carrier's lack of armament – other than the usual door guns – meaning it had "slick" sides.

The helicopters were there to help support the troops on the ground. They would bring the troops in, put them on their landing zones (LZs), and lift off for another load. The relatively slow-moving aircraft could loiter over an area, giving heavy fire support to the troops that they had just put into harm's way. Slicks would come in to pick up the troops after the mission was over. Or the same kind of birds would come in and medevac the wounded out to combat hospitals. Many of the troops who served in Vietnam feel they owe their lives to the men who crewed those birds, and came and got them when they most needed help.

The door gunner in a Huey UH-1D "slick" in Vietnam in 1965. He is armed with an M60 machine gun with the bipod legs removed. The bipod mounting lugs are still in place behind the flash hider of the weapon. The weapon is suspended by a bungee cord from the top of the door frame. This allows for maximum flexibility with the weapon. The ammunition is fed through a feed chute extending from a large ammunition box the gunner is sitting on. The gunner holds a rank of Specialist 5 according to his sleeve insignia. On his chest is a set of helicopter crewman's "chicken plate" body armor in a dark green cloth carrier. He is wearing a set of black leather glove shells to protect his hands. On his head is a green helicopter crewman's helmet with the black boom-mike extended out from the left earpiece to in front of the gunner's mouth. The visor of the helmet is slid up underneath the top of the body and locked in place. (NARA)

In April 1968, a Seawolf helicopter gunship circles over a canal in the Mekong Delta. The UH-1B Iroquois is providing support for a US Navy River Patrol Boat (PBR) operating in the area. The outboard mounts for the M16 weapons system can be seen on either side of the helicopter. Sitting inside the open door on the left side of the bird is one of the door-gunners, holding his M60 machine gun cradled in his lap. (US Navy)

Ground use in Vietnam

There were hundreds of M60 machine guns in various configurations serving in the air in Vietnam, but it was the troops on the ground, the "grunts," who used them by the thousands. At a minimum, the Table of Organization and Equipment (TO&E) for a standard infantry rifle company called for the issue of six M60 machine guns. Each of the three 42-man rifle platoons was authorized a weapons squad of two machine guns operated by a team of three men – the gunner, assistant gunner, and ammunition carrier.

The enemy in Vietnam had few armored vehicles, and these vehicles showed up only rarely during the war. So in Southeast Asia, the two 90mm recoilless-rifle gunners also in the weapons squad would usually leave their M67 recoilless rifles behind and either pack more ammo for the M60s, or pick up a third machine gun. That allowed for three machine-gun teams per platoon, or one gun for every squad in a standard rifle company. In an AirCav rifle platoon, each of the four squads of 11 men had an M60 team.

It was the M60 that gave a base of fire to each squad. That meant the weapon could be fired in support of the squad as they approached an objective. The machine-gun fire kept the enemy occupied with their own survival rather than effectively shooting back at the Americans. The most accurate method of firing the M60 was to have it mounted on the M122 tripod, but this was a piece of equipment that was left behind at a base more often than it was taken on a patrol. The M60's integral bipod usually proved more than enough of a mount to fire the weapon effectively. The big advantage of the M60 was that it could be carried and fired on the assault. A strong man could hold the M60 up and aim it like a rifle, pouring fire directly at the enemy, while a well-trained and experienced gun crew with a bipod-mounted M60 could do a lot of damage. The 7.62mm NATO round would chop through most kinds of obstacles. Even mud and earth bunkers could be damaged by the weapon. An M60 round had no difficulty smashing through a cinder-block wall while still remaining lethal.

48

In 1968, American paratroopers of the 101st Airborne Division fire back at North Vietnamese Army troops during Operation *Carentan II*. Brass can be seen coming out of the M60 being shoulder-fired by the gunner. The assistant gunner is holding the ammunition belt up high to help it feed smoothly into the weapon. The men are fighting north of Phu Bai, South Vietnam. (NARA)

During a combat indoctrination course in Vietnam, this soldier gets some trigger time on the M60 machine gun. The course is being conducted in January 1968, at the Lei Khe Base, about 40 miles north of Saigon. The muzzle blast is kicking up a cloud of dust in front of the weapon as it is fired. A piece of brass has just been ejected, a copper-colored blur above the gunner's right hand. A large pile of M13 links is scattered across the ground while the empty brass has been thrown further away from the weapon. (NARA)

There were problems, however. The M60's feed cover was made of stamped aluminum and could be bent and damaged enough to take the weapon out of action. If their support lugs were snapped the bipod legs could dangle, as they were not able to be locked in the up or down position. Other bugs were addressed, one of the most serious being a weak point where the sheet-metal receiver was welded to the machined trunnion block. By 1967, a special gauge to check a receiver was developed and issued to small-arms maintenance units in the field. Guns that didn't meet specification had to be pulled out of the line and repaired. From about this

The M4 bandoleer attached to the hanger on the side of an M60 machine gun in place to feed ammunition into the weapon. The M60 is mounted on an M122 tripod; one of the controls to the traverse and elevation mechanism is the round knob visible under and behind the pistol grip of the weapon. (US Government)

time, new-manufacture weapons were given a series of welds to eliminate what was called the "receiver stretch" problem.

The main difficulty with the M60, though, centered on a long-standing problem within the US military – a lack of trained personnel. The M60 required a crew of two in order to operate it properly, but it worked best with more. The basic team that supported a machine gun included a gunner, assistant gunner, and at least one ammunition bearer. The gunner carried the weapon and a basic load of about 300 rounds of ammunition; he was also armed with an M1911A1 pistol for his personal defense. The assistant gunner carried the spare barrel bag with its components, the T&E gear and mount, and another 300 rounds of ammunition, while the ammunition bearer carried the tripod and up to 900 rounds of ammunition; both the assistant gunner and ammunition bearer also carried M16 rifles.

The M60 needed a dedicated and well-trained crew to use the weapon to best effect. Yet in training and in combat the big gun was often handed to the newest guys to carry. It was a heavy, therefore unpopular, weapon to carry on patrol. Assistant gunners were traded off even more often than the M60 gunners, taken from their position and moved to being a regular infantryman as the need came up. Then a new man to the unit would be assigned to be the assistant gunner. Assigned ammunition bearers were often taken from the machine-gun team and added to the rifle squad to make up for shortages in personnel. Furthermore, troops developed the habit of carrying the ammunition in bare belts wrapped around their bodies, increasing the chances of dirt and debris being picked up by a loose belt and carried into the mechanism of the weapon when it was fired.

Another problem with the M60 was that to reach its full potential it needed to be employed tactically as a machine gun, not a big rifle. The capability of the weapon to be hip- or even shoulder-fired easily was a leftover from the original squad automatic weapon, the M1918A2 BAR. The M60 had a long range, and tremendous power. It could chop a position apart, fell trees, and remove cover. It felt great to handle that big weapon and feel the power as it put out rounds. So it tended to be used as a heavy automatic rifle, rather than a machine gun laying down a base of fire.

The manpower issue was never an easy one to answer. Even during the days of the active draft, there was always a shortage of men. The scarcest men available were those with the most training and experience. Although a fully trained gunner could achieve a highly effective application of fire with his M60, training time was always in short supply. This meant that if a trained man was assigned to the M60, it was the duty of the sergeant, on direction of the officer, to make sure that assignment stayed with that individual. A good M60 gunner always fired his weapon in bursts of three to five shots, to keep the rounds on target – even the M60 could be driven off target by recoil and the forces of firing, so long bursts were discouraged. Hip shooting, so-called instinctive fire, took a lot of experience to make a gunner proficient in hitting the target when firing in such a manner. Such experience would come to a man after carrying the M60 for months at a time in combat. They knew their weapon, maintained it properly, and fired it as if it were a part of them. A good M60 gunner could literally save a unit, such was the power of the weapon.

Special-operations use

The Vietnam War saw the extensive development and use of SOF by the US military. These included the men of the Navy SEALs (Sea, Air, and Land Teams), Studies and Observation Group (SOG), Long Range Reconnaissance Patrols (LRRPs), Rangers, and US Army Special Forces (USSF), among others. These groups of men, operating in teams as small as two, would go deep into territory where the enemy felt safe, and used any weapon that added to their firepower.

The small teams favored by these units only survived by controlling their contact with the enemy. The ambush was a favored tactic since it could overwhelm an enemy force quickly and allow the operators to maintain dominance of the situation. Explosives worked well for this purpose, but the other preferred weapon was the belt-fed machine gun with lots of ammunition.

The M60 was the heaviest piece of firepower that could be carried along by the SOF. The only bigger weapon they had at their disposal was the artillery fire support they could call in over their radios. But many of the missions performed by the SEALs, SOG, LRRPs, and the like operated where they couldn't call in fire. That was where the heavy punch of the M60 proved of greatest value.

Almost every member of his unit within sight is carrying ammunition belts for the M60 machine gun held by the gunner in the center of this picture. He has a bandoleer attached to the weapon and another short section of belt dangling down from the weapon. In spite of being referred to as "light," the weight of the M60 drags down the gunner's arms. The unit is conducting a house-to-house search of a village near Saigon in May, 1968. This action is part of the final mopping-up operations that followed the 1968 Tet Offensive. (NARA)

An element of Navy SEALs during their combat deployment in Southeast Asia. The men are carrying a wide variety of weapons and ammunition. Notable is the chopped SEAL-style M60 machine gun held by the standing man on the right in the picture. His weapon is fitted with the canvas and metal magazine to hold an ammunition bandoleer in place on the gun. There are three other belt-fed machine guns in the element, all Stoner 5.56mm light machine guns. But the power of the ammunition it fired helped guarantee a spot for at least one M60 with the element. (US Navy)

The men of an SOF unit couldn't afford to take anything extraneous on a patrol. The M60 packed a big punch, but it was also a heavy chunk of firepower – and not just in terms of what it spit out towards the enemy. During enemy attacks on forward operating bases, special-operations men would swing the big M60s like a rifle, cutting down the enemy all around them. Both officers and enlisted men had a healthy respect for the big gun and learned how to handle it properly.

Practice required more than just range time. Drills helped instill the actions the unit would use in most of the encounters they could expect to run into. And the applications of the big M60 were integrated into these drills. The team practiced reacting to incoming enemy fire, taking cover while giving covering fire to each other. Breaking contact with the enemy was basically a very organized form of running away, peeling off and moving while shooting. The M60 had to be placed properly so that the rest of the unit would know where it was and avoid crossing in front of their major piece of firepower. The trooper with the M60 had 500 rounds of ammunition as his personal load-out for the gun. An additional 500 rounds were distributed among the other members of his unit. Combat drills and immediate action practice also included passing that extra ammunition

The chopped M60 (opposite)

During a night ambush on a known enemy water crossing, this US Navy SEAL covers his field of fire with a "chopped" M60 machine gun. Ever mindful of the mud and dirt that could jam his weapon, this SEAL machine gunner has laid out his loose ammunition belt on a ground cloth he brought along for the purpose. The 100-round bandoleer he has hanging on the left side of his weapon is held in reserve. If the SEAL element had to break contact and run, the bandoleer would be used to feed the machine gun while on the move. Breaking contact with the enemy does not appear to be a likely problem with the lethal efficiency of the SEALs' ambush on the armed Viet Cong in the sampan.

over to the M60, wherever it would be. The weapon was a valuable asset, but that value dissipated quickly if the gun didn't have any ammunition.

The Navy SEALs, SOG, and other units quickly picked up the M60 after beginning combat operations in Southeast Asia. They liked the weapon a great deal, but found a drawback. Even though the weapon was called an LMG, after experience in moving through the jungles and wetlands, it wasn't considered light enough. The SOF were given a great deal of leeway in adapting their weapons for operations, and the M60 was no exception. They immediately abandoned the M122 tripod except for base-defense purposes. The SEALs never even took their tripods with them when they deployed. In spite of the M60 being capable of engaging targets at 1,100yd, the average engagement range during SOG patrols or a SEAL ambush was 25–30yd maximum. Even the bipod wasn't needed at these ranges; it was simply excessive weight, so was removed. The barrel was too long and the front sight unnecessary, so the barrel was cut back to the gas system. The flash of the cut-off barrel was heavy and could give away a position, so the muzzle of the shortened barrel was rethreaded and the flash hider installed again. With the front sight missing, the rear sight was superfluous and often removed. Finally, the butt stock assembly was taken off and the rubber boot from an M60B installed in its place.

The final result was the "cut-down" or "chopped" M60, a short, nasty belt-fed blaster that could rip an enemy patrol, sampan, or hootch (bamboo-mat building) to pieces. What had been a crew-served weapon was now one for a single man to operate and carry. The M60 had gone from being a 31lb weapon to a 27lb gun, both loaded with a 100-round belt. The SEALs, because of their consistent operations in a wet environment, returned to carrying the ammunition for their chopped M60 in the magazine. The heavy canvas magazine protected a chipboard box and a cloth bandoleer from the water. And if the box disintegrated from the moisture, the canvas magazine kept the belt in position for use and fed it into the weapon.

Like so many other troops in Vietnam, the SOF often removed the ammunition belts from their boxes and wore them wrapped around their bodies. It provided another easy way to carry the ammunition, as the bandoleer boxes simply wouldn't stand up to the water environment. For an ambush, particularly next to a canal or other waterway, the M60 gunner would take his belts and lay them out on a cloth for use. The cloth would keep the belts out the mud and he could feed them into the weapon over the canvas magazine. If the situation turned "fluid" and the operators had to move quickly to break contact, the M60 gunner could switch from the long belt on the ground to the one in the magazine very quickly, giving him a good 100 rounds to depend upon while moving out.

The lack of sights on the cut-down M60

An Australian trooper operating with a SOG (Studies and Observations Group) unit fires a modified M60 machine gun from the hip. The weapon has been slightly lightened by having the bipod removed from the barrel. Australia was one of the first US allies to adopt the M60 machine gun. (US Navy)

also wasn't a handicap. Operators were very practiced with their weapons and instinctive fire – where the weapon is pointed at a target rather than directly aimed – was a developed skill. For longer ranges, they commonly used tracers to direct the gunner's fire.

SEALs

The Navy SEALs put the M60 to heavy use in Vietnam. From the automatic-weapons men who would carry the big gun in their fire teams to the support boats that mounted multiples of the guns, the M60 could be seen everywhere the SEALs operated. The extremely powerful .50-cal M2 machine gun was found to be excessively heavy and its ammunition took up too much room in a number of SEAL support craft. So the HMG was removed and M60s installed in its place. Another boat used by the SEALs a lot in the latter years of the Vietnam War was the SEAL Team Assault Boat or STAB. This small watercraft positively bristled with weapons, most of them being M60 machine guns. Because of the layout of the craft, the M60D was the preferred model to be mounted. The latter, and more numerous, version of the STAB was used for a number of missions besides supporting the SEALs, and the meaning of the acronym changed to Strike Assault Boat.

For their maneuvering units – the platoon, squad, and fire team – the SEALs found the M60 to be a very important addition to their firepower. The big guns were heavy, though. The SEALs addressed that problem with the common adoption of the chopped M60. The short, handy M60 became something of a trademark for them. In every squad, there was at least one automatic weapons man armed with an M60 – they were usually big men who carried heavy loads of ammunition. For a patrol, 500 to 800 rounds was considered a large load. For ambushes or missions where they expected a major fight, there were SEALs who carried 3,000 rounds of ammunition in with them.

SEALS proved to be very inventive in addressing the ammunition-supply problems they faced. For example, to feed his machine gun for a good length of time, H– manufactured a U-shaped aluminum canister that would hold a 500-round belt of ammunition and feed it directly into his weapon. To carry his rig, H– fixed a harness to the aluminum belt box that would hold the whole mess around his waist like a thick belt while still feeding the ammunition belt into the side of his M60. (Dockery 2004b: 286)

Other SEALs developed their own methods of transporting large amounts of ammunition. One such method was to take the 600-round ammunition box from the M23 armament sub-system from a Huey door-gunner, complete with its belt chuting, and hang the box from a standard pack frame. The chuting would guide the ammunition into the left side of the chopped M60 and be secured with the same magazine bracket as on the M60D. That gave a SEAL an ammunition supply sufficient for one solid minute of firing – not something that they would normally do. But it was comforting to know that there was enough ammunition immediately available to destroy completely whatever was in front of them in terms of enemy troops.

A SEAL Team Assault Boat slips into the shore, each member of the SEAL element aboard aiming his weapon outboard. Two M60 machine guns are visible in the picture, one mounted on the gunwale of the boat on the right side in the picture, the other in the hands of a SEAL on the opposite side of the boat. (US Navy)

The Brown-Water Navy

There was another Navy organization that used the M60 in much greater numbers than the SEALs. These were the men who manned the river-patrol boats and other surface craft that made up the "Brown-Water Navy," the small (31ft) boats that moved about in the myriad watercourses of South Vietnam – the Mekong Delta in particular. The average Patrol Boat, River (PBR) had at least two .50-cal machine guns in the front gun tub of the boat, one or two M60s in the waist, and another .50-cal on the stern pedestal mount. Serving in Vietnam from March 1966, these fast-moving fiberglass gunboats moved in to wherever they were needed, often supporting SEAL missions, and opened up with roaring firepower at point-blank range. The PBRs and the four-man crews that manned them were extremely well thought of by the Navy SEALs in Vietnam.

Other surface craft operating in the waterways of Vietnam included the all-aluminum, 50ft Patrol Craft, Fast (PCF), also known as the Swift boat. Swift boats had a particular piece of firepower unique to them at the beginning of their service, in October 1965. This was the Mark 2 81mm mortar with a .50-cal M2 machine gun mounted on top of it. This firepower was very flexible in its applications. The idea was so well thought of that a version was made for the much smaller PBRs. On the rear pedestal mount of the PBR could be mounted the Mark 4 60mm mortar. This trigger-fired mortar could be aimed and fired like a cannon directly at targets, or the mortar could be cranked up and used in the classic indirect lobbing-fire mission. To complete the firepower package, the top of the Mark 2 mortar often had an M60 machine gun mounted on it. That over/under M60/60mm mortar was one of the most distinctive weapon mounts for the M60 machine gun of the entire Vietnam War.

Aboard a River Patrol Boat (PBR), a sailor fires a long burst from a mounted M60 machine gun into the shore area in the distance. The weapon is placed on one of the amidships mounts of the 31ft PBR, feeding from a large ammunition box probably sitting on the deck. Visible on the left side of the weapon is the dark, rounded shape of a C-ration can attached to the magazine bracket of the gun. The long ammunition belt is bouncing up and over the can as it feeds into the weapon. Fired brass and empty links are a blur as they exit the right side of the M60. The sailor's helmet has the expression "SAT CONG" (Kill Communists) written on the cover, a common motto among the Brown-Water sailors. (US Navy)

A new tank weapon – the M60E2

Essentially a modified M60C, the M60E2 was developed in 1967 and was intended to act as a coaxial machine gun in tanks, initially the M60 series of main battle tanks. (The coaxial gun is located in the turret of the tank, next to the main gun, and acts as an antipersonnel and antimateriel weapon.) The problem with a weapon being mounted in this way is that the turret is an enclosed environment when the tank is buttoned-down for combat, and the fumes from a firing machine gun can quickly overcome a crew.

The electric solenoid trigger of the M60C was retained for the M60E2. An extended chain-and-grip operating handle projected from the rear of the weapon, and was used to cock the gun in very confined areas. The biggest modification to the M60E2 was to the barrel. An exhaust was added to the gas system that moves expended gas forward. A long barrel shroud was added to the muzzle and the gas exhaust tube run along underneath the shroud. Now when the gun was fired from inside a tank turret, the propellant gases were mostly exhausted forward and out of the inside of the tank.

Applying the lessons of Vietnam

The close of the United States' involvement in the Vietnam War did not bring an end to the use of the M60 machine gun in US service. Thousands of the

A left-side view of the M60E2 fixed machine gun as used in various armored vehicle mounts. The long front portion of the barrel extension and thinner tube below it help guide the muzzle blast and gases out of the front of the vehicle. The large cylinder of the electric solenoid trigger at the bottom center of the receiver has a small sheet-metal manual trigger mounted underneath it. Just visible behind the weapon is the handle of the charging system that allows the weapon to be cocked from the rear. (Saco Defense)

weapons had been produced and successfully used during the war. Yet many M60s were worn down from hard use, and some weaknesses in the design had been revealed. The US military was still sensitive about difficulties with weapon designs, owing to the problems with the M16 that arose when the weapon was issued in huge numbers. Any reliability problems could cause troops to lose faith in their basic tools, even when those difficulties could be traced back to something other than the design of a weapon.

Complaints had been voiced by troops that the M60 was heavy and unreliable, and that it jammed when it was dirty, alongside other malfunctions. Once of the worst of these malfunctions was a failure to extract. Instead of pulling the fired casing out of the chamber of the weapon and ejecting it, the extractor would sometimes rip through the rim of the case, leaving it in the chamber and preventing the M60 from firing again until the barrel had been cleared or changed.

In spite of such criticisms, the M60 machine gun served with distinction in Vietnam and throughout Southeast Asia. It remained the basic machine gun of the US armed forces after the war was over. The weight and other aspects of the basic M60 machine gun were still considered major drawbacks to the design. Being a mobile strike force, the Marine Corps was particularly concerned with weight. Specifically, they wanted a lighter, more dependable M60. An additional requirement was that the "new" weapon be an advanced version of the M60, one whose changes could be applied to older weapons already in inventory. The motivation for the conversion requirement is easy to understand – it saved money.

During their nearly seven years of combat in South Vietnam, members of the "Screaming Eagles," the 101st Airborne Division, fired the M60 machine gun at the enemy countless times. In December 1972, this machine-gunner is once more putting out heavy fire with "the Pig." His assistant gunner is holding up a long belt of ammunition to help keep it out of the dirt and feed it into the weapon. (NARA)

NEW MODELS, NEW CONFLICTS

The M60E3

In 1977 Saco Defense, who had been manufacturing the
M60 since 1960 as Saco-Lowell, examined the needs
of the Marine Corps and the possible changes that
had been suggested for the M60 over its first two
decades of service. A number of the Marine
Corps' requirements had been corrected in the
older weapon and Saco took that as a starting point.

One problem involved the gas system. The original gas
piston had one open end and one sealed end. Only if the
sealed end faced back towards the receiver could it press on the
operating rod and operate the weapon properly. If the gas piston was
installed backwards, the gun would fire one round and then cease
operating. The gas-piston problem had been addressed in the M60E1, but
that weapon had never been adopted.

The M60E3 fitted with the long
barrel option. (Saco Defense)

For the new model, the barrel assemblies were lightened by removing
the bipod; a new lightweight bipod was attached to the gas-cylinder tube on
the front of the receiver. The barrels were made thinner and lighter with a
redesigned flash hider that was much smaller than the original. The Stellite
liner of the barrel was longer and would better protect the steel of the barrel
from the heat of firing, giving the assembly an extended accurate life.

The barrels were now made in two lengths. One barrel was of standard
length, 22in, with a short flash hider. The other, "commando" barrel
had a length of only 17.28in, a variation held over from the days of the
"chopped" M60s in Vietnam. Another change to the barrels involved the
front sight. In the original M60, the windage was corrected only at the rear
sight. When barrels were changed, the gunner had to remember his windage
setting for the new barrel and dial it in to his sight for maximum accuracy.
This adjustment between barrels almost never happened, however, and the
resultant loss in accuracy was just accepted. The new barrel design had a

Their concern etched on their
faces, these two Marines man a
mounted M60 machine gun in a
guard bunker at the Beirut
International Airport in December
1983. Open boxes of ammunition
lay ready to be used in their
weapon as the Marines remain
very watchful. It has only been six
weeks since 220 of their fellow
Marines were killed in a truck
bomb attack at the Marine
Barracks in Beirut. The attack
resulted in the single largest loss
of life in the US Marine Corps
since the invasion of Iwo Jima in
1945. (US Department of Defense)

windage adjustment in the front sight. Both barrels could be zeroed to the weapon so that either barrel would shoot to the same point of aim.

A further change in the barrels was that the carry handle was moved from the receiver to the barrel. Now the handle could be used to change a hot barrel, eliminating the need for the asbestos mitten, and during a barrel change the weapon could be supported on its bipod. The feed cover was changed so that it could be closed with the bolt in either the forward or rear (cocked) position. The butt stock was made of plastic and was much lighter. Corrections were implemented to the trigger mechanism as well as the operating rod, driving spring, and driving-spring guide. And a forward grip was added that made the new weapon much faster and easier to handle by the gunner.

The new weapon was the M60E3. It was adopted by the Marine Corps in 1985. Besides the basic weapon, a set of parts was assembled that could be added to the standard M60 and take it to the E3 configuration. The M60E3 conversion kit was made up of 14 components. The only change that had to be done on an original M60 to allow it to accept all of the conversion parts was a small indent drilled into the gas-cylinder tube.

Drawbacks with aspects of the new weapon were almost immediately apparent. The major complaint was that the lighter-weight barrels could

His body armor secured in place, this Marine peers at a distant object through his binoculars. He is manning an M60 mounted inside of a sandbagged bunker in Beirut. The Marine is part of the multinational peacekeeping operation in Lebanon, photographed in early November 1983. (US Department of Defense)

not be fired as long as the original heavier barrels. Instead of a firing schedule calling for a barrel change for safety after 200 rounds had been fired in one minute (rapid rate), the barrel of the M60E3 had to be changed after only 100 rounds had been fired in one minute.

The M249 SAW enters the picture

The US Army never adopted the M60E3, except for small numbers of the weapon that went to SOF units. The modifications that resulted in the M60E3 had been done to fit Marine Corps requirements rather than suggestions put forward by the Army. Instead of modifying the M60, the US Army went with a new class of machine gun. In February 1982 the US Army adopted the Fabrique Nationale-designed and manufactured M249 5.56mm machine gun as the new Squad Automatic Weapon (SAW). When the weapon entered full service in 1984, the M249 gave a belt-fed sustained-fire capability to the standard Army infantry squad while removing the weight "penalty" of issuing an LMG chambered for a full-sized rifle cartridge.

The idea of using a 5.56mm belt-fed weapon at the squad level had been tested and considered by the US Army since the middle of the 1960s, but no new designs had passed the strenuous testing required by the Army. Even though the Stoner M63A1 LMG, another belt-fed 5.56mm weapon, had seen consistent use by the Navy SEALs during the Vietnam War, the Army felt that the design couldn't meet their needs. With the adoption of the M249 SAW, more firepower could accompany a small unit while the heavier M60 remained in a support role. For the 1980s and into the 1990s, the M60 remained the primary sustained-fire LMG for the US military and US allies.

The Americas and Operation *Desert Storm*

With an increase in communist and terrorist group actions in El Salvador, Nicaragua, and elsewhere in Central America, the United States stepped up its presence in the area, particularly in Honduras. Seeking a stable base

During Operation *Desert Shield* in December 1990, this MP mans a mounted M60 machine gun overlooking a military base in Saudi Arabia. (US Department of Defense)

for operations, the United States poured aid into Honduras and, more covertly, into El Salvador. For Honduras, this aid included military support and training. US troops would help increase the capabilities of the Honduran military, which was increasingly armed with US-made weapons, including the M60 machine gun.

By the end of the 1980s the USMC used the M60E3, while the Army remained wedded to the standard M60, which was now entering its fourth decade of frontline service. One of the peak actions the United States took in Central America in this period came in the form of Operation *Just Cause*, the invasion of Panama in December 1989. Large numbers of American troops swooped down on Panama after its dictator, Manual Noriega, defied international law and took a number of American personnel hostage. Besides significant numbers of ground troops employing the M60 as part of their standard armament, several SOF units as well as the Marines employed the M60E3.

The standard M60 was in US Army hands when Coalition forces swept across the sands of the Arabian Peninsula to help throw Saddam Hussein's forces out of Kuwait when it was invaded by Iraq in the middle of 1990. The weapon did exemplary duty even in the desert environment, as long as it was kept clean and maintained by the users.

Improving the M60E3

A Product Improvement Program (PIP) had been initiated in the late 1980s to correct deficiencies in the M60E3 and improve the design and performance. By 1991, the new M60E3 (Enhanced) (also called the M60E3 PIP) was ready for issue. The new modifications brought back the original outline for the heavy barrel, increasing the weapon's ability to handle heat. Improvements were also made in parts of the gas system to make it easier to maintain. And the front heat shield had taller sides added to it to protect the gunner from a hot barrel.

To account for the barrel having a carrying handle, the fore-end assembly had been removed and a U-shaped heat shield with an open top added. This was also much like what had been done with the M60E1. The tall sides of the front heat shield extending above the barrel provide the easiest way to recognize an M60 (Enhanced) weapon. The new parts were also released as a kit to allow for the upgrading of existing weapons, but were not ready in sufficient numbers to serve during *Desert Storm*.

Somalia and Haiti

In the limited-war environment of Somalia during Operation *Restore Hope* in 1992–93, the M60 was employed. Though the US forces were restricted in their rules of engagement, the M60 still made a psychological impact with both the American and Somali forces. The appearance of an M60, with its shining belt of ammunition showing a lethal sustained-fire capability, likely helped break up some crowds of Somali rioters even when a shot wasn't fired. After the battle of Mogadishu in October 1993, when

several American helicopters were shot down and 18 US troops killed, Somalis quickly learned that the Americans were now much more prone to shoot back, and the M60 could do a lot of the firing.

Though they were not actively used, the simple appearance of the M60 likely had a subduing effect on mobs, and could help protect troops. This could be seen in Haiti during Operation *Uphold Democracy* in 1992 and 1993.

The M60E4

Continuing with their program of upgrading the M60 design, Saco Defense came up with the M60E4 series in 1994. This was an improvement of the entire family of M60 machine guns, including the M60E4 LMG, M60E4 mounted (M60D) and M60E4 coaxial (M60E2). Major modifications in the new series of weapons included a thick-walled barrel for sustained firing and a lightweight bipod that could be operated by the gunner with one hand. A redesigned ammunition hanger, and a feed cover with additional improvements that increased operator safety, eliminated some causes of jamming, as did a 30 percent increase in the amount of pull on the ammunition belt to draw it into the weapon. An integral Picatinny rail was put on the top of the feed cover, allowing for the addition of optical and electronic sighting systems to the weapon. Both the US Navy and the Army examined the M60E4. It was adopted by the US Navy in 1995 as the Mark 43 7.62mm machine gun for use by the Navy SEALs. It was also fielded by other special operations forces, but the primary users were the SEALs.

Saco Defense went out of the M60 manufacturing business prior to being sold to General Dynamics in 2000. Starting with Saco-Lowell and ending with Saco Defense, the same manufacturer has turned out more than a quarter of a million M60s in all configurations. The rights to

The M60E4 with accessories. The weapon has a muzzle suppressor attached that cuts back on the sound of firing. On the Picatinny rail section on top of the feed cover is attached an Elcan M145 optical sight. On the front handguard, an A/N PEQ-2 laser aiming light has been fitted on the right side Picatinny rail. The weapon is sitting in its bipod in front of an 800-round case of belted 7.62mm ammunition. The markings on the top of the box indicate that the belts are made up of four ball rounds to one tracer. (Author)

manufacture the M60 series were sold to US Ordnance, Inc., of Reno, Nevada, in 1999. US Ordnance went into production of the M60 family in 2000. That company has continued with an effort to improve the M60 and keep it on the frontlines. Their latest version of the M60E4/Mk 43 weapon includes a redesigned machined-aluminum feed cover with an integrated Picatinny rail. In addition, an aluminum Rail Interface System handguard allows for the mounting of optics, laser systems, sensors, and illuminators, to give the M60E4 a 24-hour operational capability.

Though being replaced in frontline use by the M240 series of automatic weapons, the M60 remained employed in the "War on Terror" from 2001. Many small craft of the US Coast Guard (USCG) would patrol American harbors and waterways with a mounted M60. Again in Iraq during Operation *Iraqi Freedom*, the M60 was often seen mounted on vehicles as a support weapon. The M60D remained a common sight as helicopter armament in both Iraq and Afghanistan during *Enduring Freedom* through the first decade of the 21st century.

Desert Storm (previous pages)

Bombed for months, abandoned by their leadership, and overrun by Coalition forces in a matter of days, the Iraqi forces who invaded Kuwait in 1990 had had more than enough of Operation *Desert Shield/Desert Storm*. With their hands in the air, this group of men want to surrender to the first Coalition forces they can.

At a shattered Kuwaiti building, two US Marines are startled to meet a large group of Iraqis walking up the road. While one Marine, with an M249 SAW at the easy ready, signals the group of defeated troops to stop, the other Marine maintains a very careful watch over the group with his M60E3 aimed. The 7.62mm slugs from the M60E3 would easily penetrate two or even three of the Iraqis at a time.

The leader of the Iraqi group holds up a white rag tied to the cleaning rod of an AK-47. Showing a white cloth was part of the instructions on the back of the surrender leaflet the man is holding up in his right hand. In the distance, oil wells burn.

IMPACT
The thunder of the M60

BATTLEFIELD IMPACT

When US units were on patrol, the power of the M60 could turn the tide of a combat situation rapidly. The phrase "Guns Up!" called back along a patrol line meant that there was something ahead, and the leader of the unit wanted his heaviest punch, the M60, up front and on line. The cry also meant that the M60 crew was going further forward into harm's way – everything the enemy had would be turned against an M60 position. Next to the M60 in a firefight was a very dangerous place to be.

The firepower of an M60 could be intoxicating to the gunner. A man firing that big gun could split trees, brush, and even rocks with the lethal scythe of bullets. With that roaring machine gun in his arms, it felt like nothing could stand in front of him. It took discipline to maintain fire properly with the weapon, not shoot wildly and waste ammunition. It also took a great deal of bravery to maintain a position and fire back at the enemy when he was shooting at the machine gun with everything he had available.

On July 24, 1966, the men of the 1st Platoon, Company I, 3rd Battalion, 5th Marines were conducting combat operations near the demilitarized zone (DMZ) in the far north of South Vietnam. The company was operating along a narrow jungle trail when they ran into an ambush. The enemy force was well camouflaged and heavily armed. The North Vietnamese Army (NVA) had made few incursions across the DMZ and into South Vietnam up to that point. That July, the 324th NVA Division had moved south across the border, and on July 24 they ran right into the path of the Marine platoon. The numerically superior enemy poured fire in on the Marines. The call went out to bring up more firepower. That call meant bringing up the M60.

Lance Corporal Richard A. Pittman had worked hard to enlist into the Marine Corps, and he had worked even harder to join a line outfit and go to Vietnam. Pittman had a problem – he was nearly blind in one eye. But that wasn't enough to deter him from military service, and he joined the Marine Corps.

When the call went out for firepower, Pittman quickly swapped his rifle for an M60, grabbed up several belts of ammunition, and moved forward. As soon as Pittman came close to the firefight, he started taking heavy fire from the enemy. He continued to push on, suppressing the enemy with accurate bursts from his M60. Additional fire started coming in from two enemy automatic weapons positions. Assaulting with his M60, Pittman took both positions while under fire, destroying them at point-blank range.

Pittman learned that there were additional Marines forward of his position, wounded and under heavy fire from both small arms and mortar rounds. Pittman continued up the trail an additional 50yd until he came upon the wounded Marines. Now the enemy focused directly on the resolute Marine, a force of between 30 and 40 NVA moving in with a bold frontal attack. Without any concern for his own safety, Pittman proceeded to establish a firing position for himself and his M60, right in the middle of the trail. The devastating fire he poured in on the enemy forces ripped the NVA unit apart. He continued firing until his M60 stopped, but there were other weapons around. Picking up an enemy submachine gun as well as a pistol from a fallen Marine, Pittman continued firing on the NVA forces, finally forcing them to withdraw. His ammunition completely exhausted, Pittman threw his last hand grenade at the enemy, then returned to his platoon.

The bold action by Pittman and his M60 helped stop the enemy advance against his fellow Marines with initiative, bravery, and complete devotion to his duty. He also inflicted heavy casualties upon the enemy. There was no question that it was Pittman's actions that helped disrupt the enemy attack and save the lives of many of his fellow Marines – including those wounded men who would have been overrun except for Pittman making his stand on the trail. In spite of his actions, the battle had been a costly one. Two-thirds of Pittman's company were casualties, wounded or killed by the NVA forces. On May 14, 1968, Richard A. Pittman was at the White House in Washington, DC, where President Lyndon B. Johnson presented him with the Medal of Honor.

On July 18, 1966, Melvin E. Newlin, then still a few months short of his 18th birthday, enlisted in the USMC in Cleveland, Ohio. In Vietnam in July the following year, Company F, 2nd Battalion, 5th Marines, had moved to the Nong Son Mountain in Quang Nam Province, site of the only active coal mine in South Vietnam. As a member of the 1st Platoon, PFC Newlin, all 5ft 9in and 140lb of him, pulled guard duty along with four of his fellow Marines. The duty was a common one – man the position on the perimeter of the Nong Son Outpost and maintain watch for enemy activity. The unit had only moved in that day, and the next day would be July 4, a holiday – or at least one back home.

The night of July 3 featured fireworks of a very serious kind as the Viet Cong launched a savage infantry assault on the Marines' outpost just

before midnight. The attack began with a heavy barrage of mortar shells, demolishing the position where Newlin stood watch, and seriously injuring him and killing his fellow Marines. Alone and facing an incoming horde of Viet Cong, the badly wounded Newlin propped himself against the M60 at his position and fired back.

With his machine gun, Newlin sent out a stream of 7.62mm projectiles, his accurate fire ripping through the incoming ranks. Wounded multiple times by enemy small-arms fire, Newlin nevertheless maintained his position. His constant fire turned back two enemy attempts to overrun his position. Finally, during the third assault, a grenade exploded next to Newlin, wounding him even more and knocking him into unconsciousness. Believing their way clear and the Marine in the outpost dead, the Viet Cong continued on to attack the bunkers within the outpost. They bypassed the silent position and focused on the main force of Marines. The 18-year old PFC was badly wounded. Shrapnel and bullets had ripped through his skinny frame and he was bleeding badly. But the wounds were not enough to stop the Marine.

When he regained consciousness, Newlin crawled over to his machine gun, brought it to bear on the enemy, and fired. His fire ripped into the rear of the enemy force, confusing them and spreading havoc among their numbers. Some of the enemy troops had captured an American 106mm recoilless rifle and were trying to swing the weapon around to fire on the Marines' bunkers. Seeing what the enemy was about to do with the 106, Newlin shifted his fire and scattered the gun crew, preventing them from being able to operate the heavy weapon.

In 1972, a camouflaged infantryman armed with an M60 machine gun waits quietly. The M60 is mounted on the M122 tripod with the original pintle mount. The pintle mount is a modification of the model used for the M1919A4 and A6 machine guns, the modification being the large metal platform that attaches to the base of the M60 forearm and receiver. (US Department of Defense)

With his fellow Marines safe from the fire of one of their own heavy weapons, Newlin again moved his fire back to the main enemy force. Reloading the hot machine gun as he had to, Newlin fired belt after belt into the Viet Cong. They finally had to stop their assault on the Marine bunkers and turn their attention back to the position they had thought silenced. Twice more the enemy assaulted his position and twice more the severely wounded young Marine fought them back. It was now past midnight and Newlin remained at his weapon, firing into the enemy until he finally fell himself, mortally wounded.

PFC Newlin's sacrifice had not been in vain. He had single-handedly broken up the momentum of the enemy attack and disorganized the entire attacking force. The time the enemy had to spend trying to stop his machine gun had giving the rest of the Marines a chance to organize a defense and beat off the Viet Cong's secondary attack. At the cost of his own life, PFC Melvin E. Newlin had helped save his fellow Marines. His posthumous Medal of Honor citation ended with the line: "His indomitable courage, fortitude, and unwavering devotion to duty in the face of almost certain death reflected great credit upon himself and the Marine Corps and upheld the highest traditions of the United States Naval Service." In Quantico, Virginia, the Marine Corps Warfighting Laboratory is housed in Newlin Hall, named after the 18-year-old Marine PFC who manned a machine gun in South Vietnam.

Soldiers in the US Army also recognized the firepower of the M60 and how its employment could swing the tide of battle. There were occasions where a single gun, properly handled by a dedicated individual, could dominate a battle. The battle of Dak To in November 1967 was one of those occasions. It was a savage fight that took place on Hill 875 with the 2nd Battalion, 503rd Infantry, 173rd Airborne Brigade, facing a large number of NVA soldiers. Two Medals of Honor, three Distinguished Service Crosses, and dozens of Silver and Bronze Stars were awarded after the battle and the 173rd Brigade received a Presidential Unit Citation for the brigade's actions. Several regiments of NVA, numbering nearly 6,000 men, had been infiltrating the area around Dak To for months. In November, the battle erupted.

A member of Company A, 2nd Battalion, 503rd Infantry – PFC Carlos James Lozada – was assigned as the gunner of a M60 machine gun. At 1400hrs on November 20, Lozada was manning a forward position on Hill 875 overlooking a well-defined trail when he spotted elements of what would be an entire company of NVA troops approaching his position. In front of the PFC were enemy troops, behind him his company and the paratroopers with whom he had lived and trained. Sounding the alarm, PFC Lozada opened fire with the enemy only 10yd away.

The accurate volume of fire from Lozada's M60 disrupted the initial attack. His shooting accounted for 20 enemy dead in that first wave alone. Yet the PFC knew he was in a very difficult situation. There was a large number of the enemy in front of him, trying to envelop his position. The NVA troops also launched an assault on the west flank of Company A, intending to cut the company off from the rest of the battalion.

The M60 variants

General Standard Characteristics

Caliber: 7.62mm NATO (7.62×51mm)

Operation: gas

Type of fire: full-automatic

Sights: open, leaf-type square-notch/blade, adjustable, calibrated 300m–1,200m (328–1,312yd) in 100m (109yd) increments

Sight radius: 21.15in (54cm)

Mount type: shoulder fired; integral bipod; M91 tripod (24.6lb/11.11kg) or M122 tripod with pintle and T&E gear (19.5lb/8.85kg)

Service cartridges: M80 ball 393 grains (25.5g); M62 tracer 383 grains (24.8g)

Projectiles: M80 ball: 149 grains (9.7g); M62 tracer: 141 grains (9.1g)

Muzzle velocity: M80 ball 2,800fps (853m/s); M62 tracer 2,730ft/sec (832m/sec)

Muzzle energy: 2,593ft/lb (3,516J)

Feed: flexible metal disintegrating 100-round M13 link belt, linked four M80 ball, one M62 tracer (standard): 6.51lb (2.95kg); left-side feed

Feed devices: M4 bandoleer with box and 100-round M13 link belt (6.8lb/3.08kg); M60 magazine bag (canvas) with 100-round M13 link belt (7.55lb/3.42kg); M60 magazine bag (nylon) with 100-round M13 link belt: (7.04lb/3.19kg)

Effective range: 1,200yd (1,100m)

Maximum range: 4,075yd (3,725m)

Variant	Overall length	Barrel length	Weight empty	Barrel weight	Cyclic rate of fire
M60	43.5in (110.5cm)	22in (56cm)	24.5lb (11.11kg)	9.19lb (4.17kg)	500–650rpm
M60E1	43.5in (110.5cm)	22in (56cm)	23.7lb (10.75kg)	5.88lb (2.67kg)	600rpm
M60E2*	43.5in (110.5cm)	22in (56cm)	22.4lb (10.16kg)		550rpm
M60E2 (with barrel extension)*	54.5in (138.4cm)	30in (76.2cm)	24.4lb (11.07kg)		550rpm
M60B**	43.5in (110.5cm)	22in (56cm)	21.1lb (9.62kg)	7.21lb (3.27kg)	550rpm
M60C**	43.25in (109.9cm)	22in (56cm)	23lb (10.43kg)	7.21lb (3.27kg)	550rpm
M60D	44.9in (114cm)	22in (56cm)	24.3lb (11.02kg)	9.19lb (4.17kg)	550rpm
M60 "Chopped"* **	39in (99.1cm)	17.5in (44.5cm)	20.54lb (9.31kg)	6.55lb (2.97kg)	550–600rpm
M60E3 (with long barrel)	42.4in (107.7cm)	22in (56cm)	19.5lb (8.85kg)	4.69lb (2.13kg)	500–650rpm
M60E3 (with long heavy barrel)	42.4in (107.7cm)	22in (56cm)	20.8lb (9.43kg)	5.91lb (2.68kg)	500–650rpm
M60E3 (with short barrel)	37in (94cm)	17.28in (43.9cm)	19.2lb (8.71kg)	4.31lb (1.96kg)	500–650rpm
M60E4 / Mark 43 Mod 0 (with long barrel)	42.4in (107.7cm)	22in (56cm)	23.1lb (10.48kg)	4.69lb (2.13kg)	500–650rpm
M60E4 / Mark 43 Mod 0 (with short barrel)	37.7in (95.8cm)	17.3in (44cm)	22.5lb (10.21kg)	4.31lb (1.96kg)	500–650rpm
M60E4 / Mark 43 Mod 0 (with assault barrel)	37in (94cm)	16.6in (42.2cm)	21.3lb (9.66kg)	5.91lb (2.68kg)	500–650rpm
Mark 43 Mod 1 (with long barrel)	42in (106.7cm)	22in (56cm)	20.76lb (9.42kg)	4.69lb (2.13kg)	500–650rpm
Mark 43 Mod 1 (with short barrel)	37in (94cm)	17.3in (44cm)	20.4lb (9.25kg)	4.31lb (1.96kg)	500–650rpm
Mark 43 Mod 1 (with assault barrel)	38in (96.5cm)	16.6in (42.2cm)	21.52lb (9.76kg)	5.91lb (2.68kg)	500–650rpm
M60E2 Enhanced (M60E4 coaxial)*	42.3in (107.4cm)	22in (56cm)	21.2lb (9.62kg)		500–650rpm
M60E2 Enhanced (M60E4 coaxial) (with barrel extension)*	53.3in (135.4cm)	30in (76.2cm)	23.2lb (10.52kg)		500–650rpm
M60D Enhanced (M60E4 Mounted)	42in (106.7cm)	22in (56cm)	22.4lb (10.16kg)	4.69lb (2.13kg)	500–650rpm

*No sights mounted on barrel   ** No bipod on barrel

The author shoulder-firing an M60E4. A vertical front grip has been added to the Picatinny mounting rail underneath the forearm of the weapon. Additionally, an A/N PEQ-2 laser aiming light is mounted to the right side of the forearm. An Elcan M145 optical sight had been added to the Picatinny mounting rail on the top of the feed cover. The weight of the muzzle suppressor helps stabilize the weapon when firing from the shoulder; brass can be seen just spinning out of the ejection port over the author's firing hand. Several additional pieces of fired brass as well as expended links can be seen moving through the air in the right side of the picture. Even with the weapon firing a multiround burst, the muzzle has not risen or moved off-target. (Author)

Company A was ordered to withdraw, but if Lozada withdrew to the relative safety of his unit, there would be no one to hold back the incoming surge of enemy soldiers. That would put the withdrawal of Company A in serious jeopardy. Therefore, even though he knew the enemy was closing in on three sides of the position, he told the other soldiers in his position to move back, and that he would cover for them. With a good supply of ammunition immediately at hand, PFC Lozada opened fire on the enemy only yards away.

Facing a thundering M60, the enemy knew they would have to take out the machine-gun position in front of them if they were to be successful in reaching the American forces beyond it. They opened up on the blocking position with everything they had available, while PFC Lozada returned fire. Finally, he fell, mortally wounded from the intense enemy fire trying to destroy his position. Picked up by his fellow soldiers. Lozada was finally taken away from the machine-gun position he had so valiantly defended. His actions served as an inspiration to the men who continued the four-day battle. PFC Carlos James Lozada was posthumously awarded one of the two Medals of Honor resulting from the fighting at Hill 875.

Comparisons

The M60 machine gun was adopted with the intention that it would be a companion weapon to the M14 rifle. Both the M14 and the M60 were chambered for the 7.62mm NATO round and so shared ammunition commonality. The M14 rifle only served for a relatively short time before the concept of the intermediate-cartridge assault rifle, in the form of the M16 and the 5.56mm round, supplanted it. Vietnam was the first major conflict where both the M16 and the M60 saw battle. Both weapons had praises lavished upon them, and their faults listed in detail.

Chambered for the 5.56mm round, the M16 was considered unreliable by its detractors, and underpowered by those used to a military rifle firing a "full-sized" bullet. To some, the power of the round that it fired gave the M60 its appeal. The two major rifle rounds during the Vietnam War were the 5.56×45mm on the Free World side, and the 7.62×39mm cartridge on the side of the Viet Cong and North Vietnamese. The 7.62×51mm NATO round fired by the M60 smashed past both of those projectiles.

The 5.56×45mm round was the first small-caliber, high-velocity round of ammunition used in large numbers by any of the world's militaries. The original Vietnam-era M193 ball round fired a 55-grain projectile from a 20in barrel at a velocity of 3,250ft/sec. It was most effective against soft-tissue targets, in which the high velocity of the projectile caused severe wounding, but the light bullet would not penetrate through wood, dirt, sand, and gravel as well as heavier bullets would.

The Viet Cong in South Vietnam used a wide variety of weapons, though they tried to standardize on certain calibers to help simplify supply. The 7.62×39mm round was widely used in the SKS carbine, AK-47 assault rifle, and RPD LMG, while the much more powerful 7.62×54mmR round was used in various versions of the Mosin-Nagant bolt-action rifle, particularly the M1944 carbine. But there were some machine guns in use by the Viet Cong that also used the 7.62×54mm ammunition.

The DP LMG was a 1926 Soviet design that gave good service during World War II, in spite of several limitations. The DP was loaded with a 49-round pan magazine, which only operated consistently when loaded with 47 rounds. It was also heavy, with an empty weight of 20lb and a loaded magazine weighing 6.17lb. The magazine was susceptible to damage from dents and bending, both of which would put it out of action. In 1946, the DP was modernized to take a belt-feed system and this weapon was named the RP-46. The RP-46 was heavy for its design – it weighed 28.7lb empty, but it also fired the 7.62×54mmR round. Both weapons were used by the Viet Cong/NVA and were faced by Free World forces in Southeast Asia.

The Russian 7.62×39mm M43 round put out a 122-grain projectile at 2,330ft/sec from a 16.34in barrel. It had evolved from the German idea of an intermediate cartridge, described earlier, and had a greater penetration than that of the 5.56×45mm round, primarily on account of the heavier bullet. The 7.62×51mm round was a slight modernization of the basic military rifle round that had been around since before World War I. The 7.62×51mm M80 ball round launched a 147-grain projectile at 2,800ft/sec from a 22in barrel. Like all military ammunition, the 7.62×51mm round was loaded with a pointed, full-jacketed bullet, as are the 5.56×45mm M193 ball round and the 7.62×39mm M43.

The Soviet 7.62×54mmR round was a rimmed cartridge that was originally designed in 1891. The cartridge is the Soviet equivalent of the American .30 M2 (.30-06) round but never underwent a "modernization" into the equivalent of the 7.62×51mm. The Type LPS loading of the 7.62×54mmR round puts out a 149-grain projectile at a velocity of 2,850ft/sec from a 28in barrel. The general ballistics of the round match

Comparisons

The M240 machine gun

The M240 machine-gun series has replaced the M60 family in most of the US armed services. The basic weapon has been modified into variants to fulfill specific applications, as was the M60 before it. Additionally, there is a special-operations weapon, the Mark 48, that is a further development of the M240 series.

Name	Caliber	Overall length	Barrel length	Empty weight	Feed device (weight)	Cyclic rate of fire	Mount (weight)
M240B	7.62mm NATO (7.62×51mm)	48.5in (123.2cm)	21.7in (55.1cm)	27.1lb (12.29kg)	100-rd disintegrating metallic M13 link belt in M4 bandoleer (6.8lb/3.08kg)	750–950rpm	Shoulder, bipod, or tripod fired; integral bipod, or M122 tripod with flex-mount and T&E mechanism 20lb/9.07kg)
M240E6	7.62mm NATO (7.62×51mm)	48.5in (123.2cm)	21.7in (55.1cm)	23.63lb (10.72kg)	100-rd disintegrating metallic M13 link belt in M4 bandoleer (6.8lb/3.08kg)	750–950rpm	Shoulder, bipod, or tripod fired; integral bipod, or M192 tripod with cradle and T&E mechanism (11.5lb/5.22kg)
M240C	7.62mm NATO (7.62×51mm)	41.2in (104.6cm)	24.7in (62.7cm)	22.2lb (10.07kg)	Disintegrating metallic M13 link belt in container; size depends on mount*	750–950rpm	Vehicle-mounted
M240D	7.62mm NATO (7.62×51mm)	41.2in (104.6cm)	21.7in (55.1cm)	25.7lb (11.66kg)	Disintegrating metallic M13 link belt in container; size depends on mount	750–950rpm	Set up for pintle mountings
M240G	7.62mm NATO (7.62×51mm)	48in (121.9cm)	23.7in (60.2cm)	25.6lb (11.61kg)	100-rd disintegrating metallic M13 link belt in M4 bandoleer (6.8lb/3.08kg)	750–950rpm	Shoulder, bipod, or tripod fired; integral bipod, or M122 tripod with flex-mount and T&E mechanism (20lb/9.07kg)
Mark 48 Mod 0	7.62mm NATO (7.62×51mm)	39.75in (101cm)	19.75in (50.2cm)	18.5lb (8.39kg)	100-rd disintegrating metallic M13 link belt in M4 bandoleer (6.8lb/3.08kg)	675rpm	Shoulder or bipod fired; integral bipod

RIGHT As part of Operation *Pil*, a Marine gunner stands watch with his M240G machine gun in the Watapur District, Kunar Province, Afghanistan, in October 2005. The long reach of the 7.62mm machine gun allows the gunner to maintain cover for his fellow Marines during the operation. (US Department of Defense)

*The ammunition cover and feed tray are set for right-hand feed. Components for right-hand feed can be fitted to the other members of the M240 family and the M240C can be converted to left-hand feed.

Comparisons
Foreign weapons

Name	Caliber	Overall length	Barrel length	Empty weight	Feed device (weight)	Cyclic rate of fire	Mount (weight)
RPD	7.62×39mm	40.8in (103.6cm)	20.5in (52cm)	15.6lb (7.08kg)	Non-disintegrating metallic link belt in 100-rd section in metal belt drum (5.29lb/2.4kg)	650–750rpm	Shoulder or bipod fired; integral bipod
PK*	7.62×54mmR	47.2in (119.9cm)	25.9in (65.8cm)	19.8lb (8.98kg)	Non-disintegrating metallic link belt in 100-rd section (5.38lb/2.44kg) or 250-rd belt (20.72lb/9.4kg)	650–700rpm	Shoulder or bipod fired; integral bipod
PKM**	7.62×54mmR	46.2in (117.3cm)	25.9in (65.8cm)	18.52lb (8.4kg)	Non-disintegrating metallic link belt in 100-rd section (5.38lb/2.44kg) or 250-rd belt (20.72lb (9.4kg)	650–720rpm	Shoulder or bipod fired; integral bipod
PKS†	7.62×54mmR	46.2in (117.3cm)	25.9in (65.8cm)	18.52lb (8.4kg)	Non-disintegrating metallic link belt in 100-rd section (5.38lb/2.44kg)) or 250-rd belt (20.72lb/9.4kg)	650–720rpm	Shoulder, bipod, or tripod fired; integral bipod; Stepanov tripod (9.92lb/4.5kg)
Pecheneg 6P41††	7.62×54mmR	45.8in (116.4cm)	25.9in (65.8cm)	18.08lb (8.2kg)	Non-disintegrating metallic	650rpm minimum	Shoulder, bipod, or tripod fired; integral bipod; Stepanov tripod (9.92lb/4.5kg)

* Adopted by the Soviet military in 1961   ** Entered service in 1969 as an improved PK. Lighter weight with major components made of metal stampings
† The tripod-mounted version of the PKM machine gun   †† A new version of the PK family but with a heavy, fixed barrel for increased accuracy

the 7.62×51mm M80 ball ammunition almost exactly. But the rimmed base of the Soviet round requires a fairly complex, and correspondingly heavier, feeding system.

A 100-round burst of fire from an M16 against a 4ft×4ft cinder-block wall 30yd away would cut through the wall. That same 100 rounds fired from an AK-47 would break a large hole in the wall. Fire 100 rounds from an M60 and the wall would be reduced to a pile of gravel. The 7.62×51mm round fired by the M60 has a penetrative power far above that of the 5.56mm M16 round, and considerably greater penetration and range over the 7.62×39mm AK-47 ammunition.

The heavier 7.62×51mm projectiles maintain their stability in flight for a longer distance than those achieved by lighter calibers. The M60 has an effective range of 1,200yd; the 5.56mm high-velocity projectile launched from an M16A1 has a normal effective range of 433yd, while the heavier but lower-velocity projectile fired from an AK-47 has an effective range of 330yd. But the 7.62×51mm round exacts a toll on the shooter for the range it gives – the round is more than twice as heavy as a 5.56×45mm, and nearly half again as heavy as a round of 7.62×39mm. What the soldier gets with the M60, however, is the ultimate personal firepower.

CONCLUSION

The M60, in its many variations, has now ceased being the primary 7.62mm LMG of the US armed forces, but the weapon is still seen in frontline use, primarily as a secondary weapon on US Navy ships and with the USCG. The mission of the M60 has been taken by another weapon, the 7.62mm M240B and its variants, a development of the FN MAG 58 ("MAG" standing for *Mitrailleuse d'Appui Général*, or "General-Purpose Machine Gun") used by many countries around the world. The M240B was adopted by the US Army as its basic machine gun in May 1997, replacing the M60 in Army service.

In 1994, the US Army ran an operational test of available machine guns in order to find a possible replacement for some or all of the 40,000 M60-series weapons in service at that time. The Army's original intention was to replace a number of the 7.62mm guns in service with a 5.56mm weapon that could be issued at the squad level. This role was already being met (from 1984 in the US Army and from 1985 in the USMC) by the belt-fed 5.56mm M249 SAW (in 1994 redesignated the M249 LMG). It was the power of the 7.62mm round with its range and penetration capabilities that caused a rethink and the retention of a 7.62mm weapon.

The 1994 testing involved two weapons, the M60E4 and the M240B. Even though it was heavier and more difficult to fire in the underarm and shoulder positions, the M240B was accepted by the Army. The US Marine Corps adopted the M240G at the same time, distinguishable from the B model by its lack of a front handguard. In 1995, the US Navy adopted the M60E4 as the Mark 43 LMG for the Navy SEALs, but with the Army having dropped the M60 series for the M240B in 1996, the days the weapon could be supported were limited.

In 2003, the US Navy put forward a request for a new 7.62mm LMG for the US Naval Special Warfare Command, to be used by both the SEALs and the Special Boat Units. The M60s in use were becoming more and more worn, parts were becoming depleted in inventory, and new designs had to be examined to see if they offered any real advantages. The weapon chosen in March 2003 to replace the venerable M60 in SEAL hands was the 7.62mm Mark 48 Mod 0 LMG, a variation of the basic M240 design. The Mark 48 Mod 0 and its successor, the Mark 48 Mod 1, are supplied by Fabrique Nationale Manufacturing, Inc., South Carolina.

At the time of writing the M60 continues in service, in diminishing numbers, with the US Navy and Coast Guard. But the weapon is still being manufactured, by US Ordnance, Inc., in Reno, Nevada. The final version of the M60, the M60E4, is as close to a perfected machine gun as can be made today. It is light, handy, and completely dependable. Several governments, particularly in South America, are purchasing as many M60E4 weapons as US Ordnance can produce. The company has expanded into the production of other weapons, but the M60 is still one of their flagship guns.

Since the manufacture of the M60 series has resumed with US Ordnance, significant numbers of the new weapons, particularly the M60E4, have been purchased by the following: the Chilean Air Force, the Colombian Army and Navy, the Czech Republic (for their 601st Special Forces), Denmark, the Italian Navy, Mexico, the Philippine Air Force, the Spanish Air Force, the Thai Navy, and Tunisia. The weapon has been in service with the Australian military since 1960, as well as with South Korea and Taiwan, who manufactured the M60 under license. The weapon has

At the US Ordnance plant in Reno, Nevada, a security container is being filled with newly produced M60E4 machine guns. Hundreds of the weapons will fill the container, then be boxed up for shipment to countries all over the world. (Author)

also served with a number of US-allied special-operations units. There have even been several US military units who have purchased limited numbers of the new M60s with their own funds. The M240 is considered a fine weapon and very dependable, but it is not easily handled when dismounted. The M60E4 with a short barrel is a quick, handy, one-man weapon that can chop through doors, walls, and ceilings with its 7.62mm NATO round. That makes the M60E4 still a very valuable tool for the soldiers tasked with conducting the "War on Terror" around the world.

Specimens of the M60 are on display in many of the various military museums around the USA. The weapon has traveled everywhere in the world with the US armed services, and it will continue to be known for a long time to come. The day of the Pig has not yet ended.

BIBLIOGRAPHY

Archer, Denis H. R. (1978). *Jane's Infantry Weapons*, 4th Edition. London: Macdonald and Jane's Publishers Ltd.

Chinn, George M. (1951). *The Machine Gun: History, Evolution, and Development of Manual, Automatic, and Airborne Repeating Weapons*, Vol. I. Washington, DC: US Government Printing Office.

Chinn, George M. (1953). *The Machine Gun: History, Evolution, and Development of Manual, Automatic, and Airborne Repeating Weapons*, Vol. III. Washington, DC: Bureau of Ordnance, Department of the Navy.

Chinn, George M. (1987). *The Machine Gun: Development of Full Automatic Machine Gun Systems, High Rate of Fire Power Driven Cannon, and Automatic Grenade Launchers by the United States and her Allies, following World War II, Korean Police Action, and the Vietnam Conflict*, Vol. V. Ann Arbor, MI: Edward Brothers Publishing Co.

Dockery, Kevin D. (2004a). *Navy SEALs: A Complete History from World War II to the Present*. New York, NY: Berkley Books.

Dockery, Kevin D. (2004b). *Weapons of the Navy SEALs*. New York, NY: Berkley Books.

Dugelby, Thomas, and R. Blake Stevens (1990). *Death from Above: The German FG42 Paratroop Rifle*. Cobourg: Collector Grade Publications.

Ezell, Edward Clinton (1983). *Small Arms of the World: A Basic Manual of Small Arms*, 12th Edition. Harrisburg, PA: Stackpole Co.

Gander, Terry J. (1997). *Jane's Infantry Weapons 1997–1998*, 23rd Edition. Coulsdon: Jane's Information Group Ltd.

Gunston, Bill (1977). *Helicopters at War*. Secaucus, NJ: Chartwell Books, Inc.

Hobart, F. W. A. (1972). *Pictorial History of the Machine Gun*. New York, NY: Drake Publishers, Inc.

Hogg, Ian V. (1986). *Jane's Infantry Weapons 1986–1987*, 12th Edition. Coulsdon: Jane's Information Group Ltd.

Johnson, Gary Paul, and Thomas B. Nelson (2010). *The World's Assault Rifles*. Lorton, VA: Ironside International Publishers, Inc.

Johnson, George B. (2002). *International Armament*, 2nd Edition. Alexandria, VA: Ironside International Publishers, Inc.

Jones, Richard D., and Leland Ness (2008). *Jane's Infantry Weapons 2008–2009*, 34th Edition. Coulsdon: Jane's Information Group Ltd.

Myrvang, Folke (2002). *MG34 – MG42: German Universal Machineguns*. Cobourg: Collector Grade Publications.

Page, Tim, and John Pimlott (1988). NAM: *The Vietnam Experience 1965–75*. London: Octopus Publishing Group Ltd.

Plaster, John L. (2004). *Secret Commandos: Behind Enemy Lines with the Elite Warriors of SOG*. New York, NY: Simon & Schuster.

Rommel, Erwin (2011). *Infantry Attacks*. New York, NY: Fall River Press (originally 1937).

Senich, Peter R. (1987). *The German Assault Rifle 1935–1945*. Boulder, CO: Paladin Press.

Smith, W. H. B. (1955). *Small Arms of the World: The Basic Manual of Military Small Arms, American – British – Russian – German – Italian – Japanese and all other important Nations*, 5th Edition. Harrisburg, PA: Military Service Publishing Co.

Smith, W. H. B. (1962). *Small Arms of the World: The Basic Manual of Military Small Arms, American – Soviet – British – Czech – German – French – Belgian – Italian – Swiss – Japanese and all other important Nations*, 7th Edition. Harrisburg, PA: Stackpole Co.

War Office (1929). *Textbook of Small Arms*. London: His Majesty's Stationery Office.

INDEX